The Spirit of Christmas

The Spirit of Christmas

Traditional Recipes, Crafts and Carols

CATHERINE ATKINSON,
VIVIENNE BOLTON
AND ALISON JENKINS

First published in 2009 by New Holland Publishers (UK) Ltd
London · Cape Town · Sydney · Auckland

Garfield House, 86–88 Edgware Road, London W2 2EA, United Kingdom
www.newhollandpublishers.com

80 McKenzie Street, Cape Town 8001, South Africa
Unit 1, 66 Gibbes Street, Chatswood, NSW 2067, Australia
218 Lake Road, Northcote, Auckland, New Zealand

ISBN 978 184773 640 6

Senior Editor: Louise Coe
Production: Marion Storz
Design: Silke Braun
Editorial Direction: Rosemary Wilkinson

1 3 5 7 9 10 8 6 4 2

Reproduction by PDQ Digital Media Solutions Ltd, UK
Printed and bound by Times Offset (m) Sdn Bnd, Malaysia

NOTE
The measurements for each project or recipe are given in metric and imperial.
These are not interchangeable so please use just one set of measurements.

CONTENTS

Introduction

Christmas is a special time of year when we can adorn the house with lavish decorations and take pleasure in eating special seasonal foods. There can also be great enjoyment in the production of your own unique homemade Christmas crafts and delicacies – in fact this creative process can be equally as satisfying as the final product. This book provides an array of wonderful projects for you to make and enjoy, bringing a hint of old-fashioned Christmas cheer to your home.

The recipes in this book illustrate some of the wonderful seasonal treats throughout the world. Many of these are age-old customs: from mince pies – first created more than two centuries ago, with the fruit-packed version that we know and love today becoming popular in Victorian times – to the classic German Lebkuchen cookies – soft, spicy, cleverly cut and beautifully iced Christmas treats.

Many of the cakes and bakes here can be made days or even months ahead; indeed some, such as Plum Pudding and Classic Christmas Cake, are best made many weeks before eating to allow their flavours to mingle and mature. Others are better made a little closer to Christmas and make wonderful gifts, including All-Butter Shortbread and Rich Chocolate Truffles. Welcoming Christmas drinks are also very much a part of the festive season and here you have a chance to try

Brandied Egg-Nog and a citrus-scented and spiced Mulled Wine.

The craft projects use a selection of traditional and modern craft methods to make both useful and stylish decorations. Some of these are designed for use over a single festive period, while others – for example the beautiful table napkins and the elegant padded tartan shape tree decorations – will be used again and again, thereby justifying the time spent making them. There are also gilded nuts and fruit to add a look of opulence to a Christmas mantelpiece display and pretty hand-stamped or stencilled gift wrap for personalizing your gifts. The festive paper chains and hanging garlands are also lovely simple projects that the whole family can make together and enjoy in no time at all.

We hope you will find plenty in this book to inspire you and bring forth the spirit of Christmas.

October	Make the Plum Pudding and store in the fridge or in a cool dry place. Make a Classic Christmas Cake (minus the topping) and store in a cool dry place.
	Make your Christmas cards from the Packed Christmas Stocking Cards, Festive Christmas Cards and Photographed Holly Cards. Start work on projects that may take some time to complete: your Star Tree Topper, Christmas Stockings and Organza Gift Pouches.
November	Check your Christmas table linen. Make Holly Napkins and Ribbon Napkin Rings.
	Create your Paper Lanterns and Beaded Glass Votive Holders. Check through your tree decorations and candle holders. Make any new items required, such as Tartan Padded Shapes, Felt Tree Decorations and Angel and Reindeer Tree Decorations.
early December	Send out your Christmas cards. Prepare your Decorated Paper and Gift Bags and Stencilled Star Gift Wrap.
3 weeks before Christmas	Cover your Christmas Cake with almond paste and fondant. Store in a cool dry place. Make your Paper Chains and Hanging Garlands.
2 weeks before Christmas	Bake Lebkuchen and store in an airtight tin with baking parchment between the layers.
	Buy your Christmas tree and decorate it. Hang your Paper Chains and Hanging Garlands around the house and place Paper Lanterns and Beaded Glass Votive Holders on tables or windowsills. Decorate the mantelpiece with an Angelic Mantelpiece Decoration or Gilded Fruit Mantelpiece Decoration. Hang your Snowflake Curtain. Construct your Holly Christmas Wreath and hang on the door.
5 days before Christmas	Make Mince Pies and store in an airtight container or preferably in the fridge. Make All-Butter Shortbread and store in an airtight container. Make the gingerbread pieces for your Gingerbread House and store in airtight containers.
	Wrap up all of your Christmas presents.
3 days before Christmas	Make Rich Chocolate Truffles and keep in an airtight container in the fridge. Assemble and ice your Gingerbread House. Make the pastry and purée for your Pumpkin Pie.
2 days before	Assemble and bake your Pumpkin Pie.
Christmas Eve	Decorate the Christmas table and hang up your stockings.
Christmas Day	Prepare Mulled Wine on the day; it can be kept warm for several hours. Make your Brandied Egg-Nog immediately before serving.

Recipes

Classic Christmas Cake

This traditional cake is rich, dark, delicious and packed with fruit. It improves with keeping and ideally should be made at least a month before Christmas to allow the flavour to develop and mature. You can vary the proportions and the type of dried fruit, plus include other chopped glacé (candied) fruits such as pineapple and ginger, but make sure you don't change the total quantity of dried fruit used (825 g/1 lb 13 oz). The cake can be served either un-iced or covered in almond paste and fondant icing, as suggested here.

1. Put the mixed peel, sultanas, currants, raisins, cherries and chopped almonds in a bowl and pour over the brandy, rum or sherry. Stir well to coat the fruit, then cover with clingfilm (plastic wrap). Leave to soak for at least 3 hours, or overnight if preferred, to allow the fruit to soften and soak up the alcohol.

2. Grease and line the base and sides of a deep 20 cm (8 in) round tin or 18 cm (7 in) square tin with a double thickness of greaseproof paper. Tie a double thickness brown paper band around the outside of the tin. Preheat the oven to 150°C (300°F/Gas 2).

3. In a large bowl, beat the butter and orange zest together, then add sugar and beat until the mixture has lightened in colour and is fluffy. Add the eggs and ground almonds a little at a time, beating well after each addition.

4. Sift the flours, spices and salt together, then add about a third of this mixture with a third of the fruit to the creamed mixture. Gently fold and stir until almost combined, then add the rest of the flour and fruit. Stir everything together until well mixed but do not beat.

5. Spoon and scrape the mixture into the prepared tin. Smooth the top level with the back of the spoon, making sure that the fruit is covered by the cake mixture. Lift up the tin and drop it onto the work surface to help release any air bubbles.

6. Bake the cake on the middle shelf of the oven for 1 hour, then lower the oven temperature to 140°C (275°F/Gas 1). Bake for a further $1^{1}/_{2}$–2 hours or until a fine skewer inserted into the middle of the cake comes out clean.

7. Remove the cake from the oven and leave in the tin to cool. Turn the cake out of the tin, but do not remove the lining paper as it helps to keep the cake moist. Wrap in greaseproof (waxed) paper, then wrap in foil. Store the cake

MAKES A 20 CM (8 IN) ROUND OR 18 CM (7 IN) SQUARE CAKE

- ★ 50 g ($1^{3}/_{4}$ oz) chopped mixed peel
- ★ 225 g (8 oz) sultanas
- ★ 225 g (8 oz) currants
- ★ 225 g (8 oz) raisins
- ★ 100 g ($3^{1}/_{2}$ oz) glacé (candied) cherries, quartered
- ★ 75 g ($2^{3}/_{4}$ oz) almonds, chopped
- ★ 120 ml (4 fl oz) brandy, rum or sherry
- ★ 225 g (8 oz) butter, softened
- ★ zest of 1 orange
- ★ 225 g (8 oz) soft dark brown sugar
- ★ 4 eggs, lightly beaten
- ★ 50 g ($1^{3}/_{4}$ oz) ground almonds
- ★ 225 g (8 oz) plain (all-purpose) flour
- ★ 50 g ($1^{3}/_{4}$ oz) self-raising (self-rising) flour
- ★ 1 tsp ground cinnamon
- ★ 1 tsp ground mixed spice
- ★ $1/_4$ tsp grated nutmeg
- ★ pinch of salt

FOR THE COVERING:
- ★ 4 tbsp apricot jam
- ★ 2 tsp brandy (optional)
- ★ 500 g (1 lb 2 oz) white almond paste
- ★ icing (confectioners') sugar, for dusting
- ★ 750 g (1 lb 10 oz) fondant icing

Tips

*If you prefer, use 825 g
(1 lb 13 oz) 'luxury' mixed
fruit instead of the mixed
peel, sultanas, currants,
raisins, and cherries.*

❧✺❧

*For a really moist
well-flavoured cake, 'feed'
with a little extra alcohol
after baking and cooling.
Remove from the tin, prick
the top all over with a fine
skewer and spoon over 2
tbsp of brandy (or alcohol
of your choice). Wrap and
store the cake the right way
up in a cool place for a
week. Unwrap, prick the
base and spoon over 2 tbsp
brandy. Re-wrap and store
the cake upside down (to
help flatten the top).*

in a cool place; it will keep for up to
3 months. For longer storage, freeze the
cake, making sure it is thawed before
covering with almond paste and icing.

8. To cover the cake, heat the apricot jam
in a small saucepan with 2 tsp water or
brandy until it bubbles and boils, then
sieve to remove any lumps and allow to
cool. Trim the top of the cake level if
necessary. Turn the cake over so that the
flat bottom becomes the top. Roll out
half of the almond paste on a surface
lightly dusted with icing (confectioners')
sugar to a round or square (trim the
edges straight with a knife) to fit the top
of the cake. Brush the top of the cake
with some of the apricot glaze and place
the almond paste round or square on top.

9. Place the cake on a board about 5 cm
(2 in) larger than the cake. Roll out the
remaining almond paste to a strip the
same height and perimeter of the cake
(use a piece of string to measure this).
Brush the sides of the cake with apricot
glaze, then place one end of the almond
paste strip against the side of the cake
and unroll it, gently pressing into place.
Use your fingers to smooth over the
joins of the paste. Flatten the top gently
with a rolling pin. Leave in a cool dry
place for 1–2 days to allow the almond
paste to dry.

10. Lightly knead the fondant icing until
pliable. Dust the work surface with a
little icing (confectioners') sugar. Roll

out icing into a round or square at least
5 cm (2 in) larger than the cake all
round. Using a rolling pin, lift the icing
on top of the cake, draping it over the
edges. Gently press the icing onto the
sides of the cake, then trim off the
excess icing at the base. You can now
decorate the cake as liked, using the
icing trimmings. Store in a cool dry
place for at least 2 months and no
longer than 4 months before eating.

VARIATION:
Royal-Iced Christmas Cake

You can ice the cake with 700 g (1 lb
8 ½ oz) royal icing instead of fondant
if you prefer. You can buy packets of this
at the supermarket, or you can prepare
your own. Lightly whisk 3 egg whites or
1 ½ tbsp powdered albumen prepared
following the manufacturer's instructions
and 2 tsp liquid glycerine (this stops the
icing becoming too hard) with a fork.
Using a wooden spoon, gradually add
700 g (1 lb 8 ½ oz) sifted icing
(confectioners') sugar, mixing in a few
heaped tablespoons at a time. You may
not need to add all of the sugar; the final
icing should be very thick and stand in
soft peaks if you want to spread it, or stiff
peaks for piping. Keep the icing in an
airtight container until ready to use.

Plum Pudding

The tradition of serving Christmas pudding was introduced to Victorian England by Prince Albert. Originally tied in a cloth and then boiled to create a round pudding, it was made on 'Stir Up Sunday', the Sunday before advent when all the family gave the pudding mixture a stir and made a secret wish. The name 'plum' originally referred to the prunes that were chopped and added to the mixture, but later came to refer to any dried fruit.

1. Soak the prunes overnight in the cold tea, then drain and chop them. Chop the cherries, candied peel and almonds, then quarter, core and coarsely grate the eating apple.

2. Sift the flour and spices together into a large bowl, then stir in the suet or butter, sugar, breadcrumbs, sultanas, raisins, currants, cherries, candied peel and almonds. Add the soaked prunes, apple, orange or lemon zest, eggs, beer and 1 tbsp of the brandy or rum. Mix everything together well.

3. Grease and line the base of the pudding bowl with a circle of greaseproof (waxed) paper. Spoon in the mixture and level the top with the back of the spoon. Cover the bowl with greaseproof paper and foil, pleated in the centre to allow the pudding room to rise a little. Tightly secure under the rim with string.

4. Put the pudding on a trivet or upturned saucer in a large saucepan and pour in enough boiling water to come halfway up the sides of the bowl. Bring to the boil, then reduce the heat so the water bubbles gently and cover the pan with a lid. Steam the pudding for 3 hours, checking at intervals to ensure that the pan doesn't boil dry and topping up the pan with boiling water as necessary.

5. Lift the pudding out of the pan and leave to cool, then re-cover with fresh greaseproof paper and foil. Store in a cool, dark place for at least one month and up to six months to allow the pudding to mature.

6. On the day of serving, steam the pudding as before for about 2 hours. Turn out onto a warmed serving plate.

MAKES A 1.2 LITRE (2 PINT) PUDDING TO SERVE 6–8

- ★ 100 g (3^1/$_2$ oz) prunes, stoned
- ★ 300ml (10 fl oz) cold tea
- ★ 50 g (1^3/$_4$ oz) glacé (candied) cherries
- ★ 25 g (1 oz) candied peel
- ★ 50 g (1^3/$_4$ oz) blanched almonds
- ★ 1 eating apple
- ★ 50 g (1^3/$_4$ oz) self-raising (self-rising) flour
- ★ 1 tsp ground mixed spice
- ★ ^{1}/$_2$ tsp ground ginger
- ★ ^{1}/$_4$ tsp freshly grated nutmeg
- ★ 75 g (2^3/$_4$ oz) suet or coarsely grated butter
- ★ 75 g (2^3/$_4$ oz) soft dark brown sugar
- ★ 50 g (1^3/$_4$ oz) fresh white breadcrumbs
- ★ 175 g (6^1/$_4$ oz) sultanas
- ★ 175 g (6^1/$_4$ oz) raisins
- ★ 50 g (1^3/$_4$ oz) currants
- ★ finely grated zest of 1 orange or lemon
- ★ 2 eggs, lightly beaten
- ★ 150 ml (5 fl oz) dark beer
- ★ 5 tbsp brandy or rum

BRANDY BUTTER:

- ★ 225 g (8 oz) unsalted (sweet) butter
- ★ 225 g (8 oz) light soft brown sugar
- ★ finely grated zest of 1 orange
- ★ 4 tbsp brandy

7. To make the brandy butter, cream the butter and sugar until very light. Beat in the orange zest and brandy, then chill until ready to serve.

8. Warm the remaining 4 tbsp of brandy or rum in a saucepan, pour over the pudding and set alight. When the flames have gone out, cut into wedges and serve with the brandy butter.

VARIATION:
Rum Sauce

You can serve the pudding with rum sauce, rather than brandy butter if you prefer. Melt 40 g (1 ^{1}/$_2$ oz) butter in a saucepan, add 25 g (1 oz) plain (all-purpose) flour and gently cook for 1 minute. Remove the pan from the heat and gradually stir in 450 ml (16 fl oz) milk. Return to the heat and bring to the boil, whisking all the time until thickened. Simmer for 2 minutes. Stir in 25 g (1 oz) caster (superfine) sugar and 3 tbsp rum.

Tips

If you use butter rather than the more traditional suet in this pudding, freeze it first to make grating easier.

❦

For a really dark pudding, beat the eggs with 1 tsp black treacle or molasses.

'Mrs Cratchit entered –
flushed, but smiling proudly – with the pudding,
like a speckled cannon-ball, so hard and firm,
blazing in half of half-a-quartern of ignited brandy,
and bedight with Christmas holly stuck into the top.
"Oh, a wonderful pudding!"
Bob Cratchit said, and calmly too,
that he regarded it as the greatest success achieved by
Mrs Cratchit since their marriage...'

- Charles Dickens, A Christmas Carol *-*

Mince Pies

Until Victorian times, mince (mincemeat) pies were made with finely chopped meat mixed with dried fruit and spices, hence the name. It is said that these are a favourite food of Father Christmas and one or two should be left on a plate by the chimney, along with a glass of sherry or milk and a carrot for the reindeer, on Christmas Eve.

1. Sift the flour, 1 tsp sugar and the salt into a large bowl. Rub in the butter until the mixture resembles fine breadcrumbs. Mix the egg yolk and water together along with some orange zest, if desired. Sprinkle over the dry ingredients and mix lightly to form a dough. Gather together into a ball. Knead on a lightly floured surface for a few seconds until smooth, then wrap in cling film (plastic wrap) and chill for 30 minutes before using.

2. Put mincemeat and whisky or liqueur in a bowl and stir together. Preheat the oven to 200°C (400°F/Gas 6).

3. On a lightly floured surface, roll out two-thirds of the pastry to a 3 mm (1/4 in) thickness. Using a 7.5 cm (3 in) fluted round cutter, stamp out 12 circles of pastry. Gently press these into a 12-hole patty tin; the pastry should come just a little above the tins to allow for shrinkage as they cook. Divide the mincemeat between the pastry cases.

4. Roll out remaining pastry and stamp out 12 stars, using a 6 cm (2 1/2 in) cutter.

Top each filled pastry case with a star shape. Lightly whisk the egg white with a fork until frothy. Brush the stars with a little egg white and sprinkle with remaining sugar. Bake for 20–25 minutes until golden. Leave in the tins for 5 minutes, then transfer to a wire rack. Serve warm, with icing sugar sprinkled over, if desired.

FOR THE PASTRY:
- ★ 225 g (8 oz) plain (all-purpose) flour
- ★ 2 tbsp caster (superfine) sugar
- ★ pinch of salt
- ★ 150 g (5 1/4 oz) chilled butter, diced
- ★ 1 egg, separated
- ★ 2 tbsp chilled water
- ★ finely grated zest of 1 small orange (optional)

FOR THE FILLING:
- ★ 225 g (8 oz) mincemeat
- ★ 1 tbsp whisky or orange liqueur

TO SERVE:
- ★ icing (confectioners') sugar, for sprinkling (optional)

Tip

The mince (mincemeat) pies are delicious served with a spoonful of whisky or orange-liqueur butter. To make the butter, beat 50 g (1 3/4 oz) softened butter with 75 g (2 3/4 oz) sifted icing (confectioners') sugar until light and fluffy, then beat in 1 tbsp whisky or orange liqueur and 1 tsp finely grated orange rind. If liked, let the mince pies cool, then gently lift off the stars, spoon or pipe a whirl of the flavoured butter on top of the filling, then replace stars.

All-Butter Shortbread

There are many variations for this famous Scottish bake, but all cooks agree that butter is an essential ingredient for a melt-in-the-mouth flavour. This simple version is cooked in a shallow round tin to make classic wedge-shaped 'petticoat tails'. Shortbread keeps very well and makes an excellent Christmas gift.

MAKES 8 PIECES
- ★ 150 g (5 1/4 oz) plain (all-purpose) flour
- ★ 25 g (1 oz) ground rice or rice flour
- ★ 100 g (3 1/2 oz) chilled butter, diced
- ★ 50 g (1 3/4 oz) caster (superfine) sugar, plus 1 tbsp for sprinkling

1. Lightly oil the base and sides of a loose-bottomed, shallow 20 cm (8 in) round tin. Preheat the oven to 170°C (325°F/Gas 3).

2. Sift the flour and ground rice or rice flour into a mixing bowl. Add the butter to the flour, then rub in until the mixture resembles fine breadcrumbs. Stir in the sugar. Gather the dough together with your hand and turn onto a clean surface. Knead very lightly until it forms a ball, but take care not to over-knead or the shortbread will be tough and greasy.

3. Press the mixture into the prepared tin with your fingers, then use the back of a spoon to press down the top and make it level. Prick all over with a fork (to let any moisture out of the mixture and keep it level and crisp as it cooks), then mark a pattern around the edge with the prongs of a fork. Mark the mixture into eight equal pieces with a blunt knife, cutting right through the shortbread to the base of the tin.

4. Bake the shortbread in the oven for 25–30 minutes, until a pale golden colour. Sprinkle the top with 1 tbsp sugar and leave to firm in the tin for 10 minutes. Remove from the tin (but leave the shortbread on the base) and cool on a wire rack before carefully cutting into wedges, following the marked lines. Store in an airtight tin.

VARIATION:
Sugar-Crusted Shortbread Rounds

Shape the mixture into a sausage shape about 5 cm (2 in) thick. Wrap in clingfilm (plastic wrap) and chill until firm. Sprinkle some demerara sugar onto a sheet of baking parchment. Unwrap the dough and roll in sugar until evenly coated, then slice into 1 cm (1/2 in) thick discs. Space well apart on a baking sheet and bake for 20–25 minutes. Cool on the baking sheet for 5 minutes, then transfer to a wire rack.

Lebkuchen

These cookies, with their slightly soft, chewy texture and fragrant spicy flavour, are a speciality of Nuremberg in Germany, where they are cut into fancy shapes, beautifully iced and sold in the Christmas markets.

1. Put butter and sugar in a mixing bowl and beat together until the mixture is creamy. Beat in honey and molasses or treacle, followed by the egg, a little at a time. Stir in the almonds, then sift the flour and spices over the mixture and mix together to make a firm dough. Wrap in clingfilm (plastic wrap) and chill in the fridge for 20 minutes.

2. Preheat the oven to 180°C (350°F/ Gas 4). Thinly roll out the dough on a lightly floured surface until it is a little thicker than 5 mm (¼ in). Use 7.5 cm (3 in) biscuit cutters to stamp out star and heart shapes.

3. Place on two baking sheets lined with baking parchment, leaving a little space between each to allow room to spread. Bake for about 10 minutes, or until risen; do not overcook or they will loose their soft texture. Allow to cool on the sheets for a few minutes, then transfer to a wire rack and leave until completely cool.

4. For the toppings, sift icing (confectioners') sugar into a bowl. Stir in about 1½ tbsp warm water, or enough to make a thick smooth icing. Spread this over half of the biscuits. Break chocolate into squares and melt in the top of a double boiler or in a heatproof bowl set over a pan of barely simmering water. Allow the chocolate to cool for a few minutes, then use to top the remaining biscuits.

5. When the toppings have set, store the lebkuchen in single layers interleaved with baking parchment in an airtight container. Store in a cool place and eat within two weeks of making.

MAKES ABOUT 30
- ★ 120 g (4¼ oz) unsalted (sweet) butter, softened
- ★ 120 g (4¼ oz) soft light brown sugar
- ★ 50 g (1¾ oz) clear honey
- ★ 50 g (1¾ oz) molasses or black treacle
- ★ 1 egg, lightly beaten
- ★ 50 g (1¾ oz) ground almonds
- ★ 350 g (12 oz) self-raising (self-raising) flour
- ★ 1½ tsp ground ginger
- ★ 1 tsp ground cinnamon
- ★ pinch of ground cardamom or mixed spice

FOR THE TOPPINGS:
- ★ 150 g (5¼ oz) icing (confectioners') sugar
- ★ 250 g (9 oz) plain (dark) chocolate

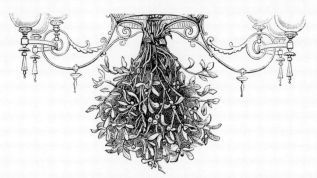

Gingerbread House

Decorated with snow-like royal icing and small colourful sweets, this charming gingerbread house can be lit from inside with a tealight to create a welcoming glow. It makes a stunning Christmas centrepiece.

1. Line 3 large baking sheets with baking parchment. Draw the templates on page 114 onto graph paper, then trace onto thin card and cut out.

2. Put the butter into a saucepan with the sugar and golden (light corn) syrup. Heat gently until melted, stirring occasionally. Set aside to cool for a few minutes.

3. Sift the flour, ginger, mixed spice and bicarbonate of soda into a bowl and make a hollow in the middle. Mix the egg yolks and milk together, then add to the hollow along with the melted butter mixture. Mix together, then gently knead the mixture on a lightly floured surface until smooth. Divide the dough into three and wrap two of the pieces in clingfilm (plastic wrap) to keep them soft.

4. Preheat the oven to 180°C (350°F/ Gas 4). Roll out the third of dough on a sheet of baking parchment on a floured work surface until it measures about 35 x 23 cm (13³/₄ x 9 in). Slide a baking sheet under the paper and dough. Place the templates for the 'end of house', the 'side of house' and the chimney pieces on the dough, leaving a little space between them and cut out. Carefully remove the excess dough. Then cut out the windows from the end and side of the house by cutting out a 4 x 4 cm (1¹/₂ x 1¹/₂ in) square. Carefully remove these pieces, cut in half and keep to make shutters (they will be attached after baking).

5. Repeat with the second piece of dough and baking sheet, cutting out a piece of dough for the other end of the house and the other side of the house. Cut out the windows and a door piece. Repeat with the third piece of dough, cutting out two 'roof' templates.

MAKES A 22 CM (8³/₄ IN) HIGH HOUSE

★ 175 g (6¹/₄ oz) butter, diced

★ 175 g (6¹/₄ oz) soft dark brown sugar

★ 3 tbsp golden (light corn) syrup

★ 700 g (1 lb 8 oz) plain (all-purpose) flour

★ 1¹/₂ tbsp ground ginger

★ 1 tsp ground mixed spice

★ 2 tsp bicarbonate of soda (baking soda)

★ 3 egg yolks

★ 135 ml (4³/₄ fl oz) milk

★ ¹/₂ quantity of royal icing (see page 12)

★ colourful sweets, to decorate (optional)

6. Bake all of the pieces in the oven for 10–12 minutes until dark golden. (It is important to make sure that the biscuits are cooked through or they won't be rigid enough.) While still warm, place the templates on the biscuits and trim back into shape if necessary (only trim one long side of each roof piece as it doesn't matter if the other sides have spread a little). Leave to cool on the baking sheets.

7. To assemble, take the ends and sides of the house and pipe royal icing along the base and side edges. Put them together on a cake board and leave to dry for 1 hour or until firm. Add the roof pieces, sticking them together with royal icing. Leave for a further hour until dry, then stick on the door, window shutters and chimney.

8. When all of the pieces are dry and firm, pipe more royal icing on the roof of the house to resemble snow. If desired, decorate the house with small colourful sweets, attaching them with royal icing. If possible, store the house in an air-tight container. Eat within four days of making.

Tips

If you are using a tealight it is easier to put it inside the house before assembling. Place it near a door or window, so that it can easily be lit with a long match.

❧

Any trimmings can be re-rolled and used to make gingerbread cookies or gingerbread men.

Silent Night

Silent night, holy night.
All is calm, all is bright.
Round yon Virgin Mother and Child,
Holy Infant so tender and mild,
Sleep in heavenly peace,
Sleep in heavenly peace.

Silent night, holy night!
Shepherds quake at the sight!
Glories stream from heaven afar,
Heavenly hosts sing Alleluia!
Christ, the Saviour is born,
Christ, the Saviour is born.

Silent night, holy night!
Son of God, love's pure light;
Radiant beams from Thy holy face,
With the dawn of redeeming grace.
Jesus, Lord at Thy birth,
Jesus, Lord at Thy birth.

- Josef Mohr -

Rich Chocolate Truffles

These are delicious served as an after-dinner treat with coffee or make a delightful Christmas gift. Because they are made with fresh cream, they should be stored in the fridge and eaten within 3–4 days of making.

1. Break the chocolate into squares, then finely chop (this is easiest in a food processor). Melt the chocolate with the cream in the top of a double boiler or in a heatproof bowl set over a pan of barely simmering water. Stir until smooth and remove from the heat. Leave to cool at room temperature for 20 minutes or until thickened.

2. Stir in rum, brandy or liqueur. Beat with an electric whisk for about 5 minutes or until the mixture has become paler in colour and fluffy; it should stand up in peaks when the whisk is lifted. Chill for 2–3 hours in the fridge until firm.

3. Decorate the truffles as desired. For rolled truffles, sprinkle a tray lined with baking paper with sifted cocoa powder, chopped nuts or chocolate sprinkles. Place even-sized heaped teaspoonfuls of the truffle mixture on the tray and quickly roll into balls. Place the truffles in individual sweet cases and chill in the fridge for at least 2 hours. For dipped chocolate truffles, roll the truffle mixture into balls, place on a tray and freeze for several hours. Melt white or plain (dark) chocolate in a small deep bowl; you'll need about 175 g (6¼ oz) for 20 truffles. Spear the truffles, one at a time, with a wooden cocktail stick, then dip into the melted chocolate, turning to coat evenly. Place on a tray lined with baking parchment. Decorate with nuts, crystallized rose petals, pieces of glacé (candied) fruit or white chocolate drops and chill until set. Alternatively, pipe a drizzle of white or plain contrasting chocolate over the top.

VARIATION:
Non-Alcoholic Truffles

For an alcohol-free version, add an extra 1 tbsp cream and a few drops of vanilla essence instead of the alcohol.

MAKES ABOUT 20 TRUFFLES
- ★ 200 g (7 oz) good quality plain (dark) or milk chocolate
- ★ 4 tbsp double (heavy) cream
- ★ 2 tbsp dark rum, brandy or favourite liqueur

TO FINISH:
- ★ cocoa powder, chopped nuts or real chocolate sprinkles (optional)
- ★ 175 g (6¼ oz) good quality white, plain (dark) or white and plain (dark) chocolate (optional)
- ★ glacé (candied) fruit, crystallised rose petals, white chocolate drops or nuts (optional)

Tip

For dipped chocolate truffles, couverture chocolate is ideal, or you can add ½ tsp groundnut oil to ordinary chocolate when melting.

Pumpkin Pie

This spicy sweet pie is a traditional American dish served at both Christmas and Thanksgiving. It is always made with just a single crust and the filling is a smooth pumpkin purée blended with eggs and cream to create a silky set custard.

1. Sift the flour and icing (confectioners') sugar into a large mixing bowl and rub in the butter until the mixture resembles fine breadcrumbs. Lightly whisk the egg and water together and sprinkle over the dry ingredients. Mix together to make a dough, then lightly knead on a floured surface for a few seconds until smooth. Wrap and chill for 30 minutes.

2. Meanwhile, put the pumpkin in a heavy-based pan. Add salt and just enough water to cover. Bring to the boil and simmer for 15–20 minutes, until tender. Drain well, then mash until very smooth. Spoon the purée into a fine sieve and set over a bowl to drain.

3. Roll out the pastry on a lightly floured surface and use to line a 23 cm (9 in) loose-bottomed fluted flan tin. Chill for 15 minutes. Meanwhile, put a baking sheet in the oven and preheat to 200°C (400°F/Gas 6).

4. Prick the base of the pastry all over with a fork, line with baking parchment or foil and baking beans and place on the hot baking sheet. Bake for 10 minutes, then remove the paper or foil and beans and cook for 5 more minutes. Lower the oven temperature to 190°C (375°F/Gas 5).

5. While the pastry case is baking, make the filling. Put the pumpkin purée in a bowl and stir in the eggs, sugar, syrup, cream and spices. Pour into the pastry case and bake for 35–40 minutes, until the filling is lightly set. Transfer the tin to a cooling rack and leave until just warm. Remove the pie from the tin, dust generously with icing (confectioners') sugar and serve warm.

Tips

Butternut squash makes a good alternative when pumpkin is unavailable. The flesh is slightly denser, so doesn't need draining after puréeing.

❧

Pastry holly leaves make an attractive decoration on top of the pie. Cut these from re-rolled pastry trimmings and bake separately on a baking sheet for 10–12 minutes while cooking the pastry case. Arrange on top of the pie before serving.

SERVES 8

FOR THE PASTRY:

- ★ 225 g (8 oz) plain (all-purpose) flour
- ★ 2 tbsp icing (confectioners') sugar
- ★ 100 g (3½ oz) butter, diced
- ★ 1 egg
- ★ 1 tbsp chilled water

FOR THE FILLING:

- ★ 900 g (2 lb) pumpkin to yield 675 g (1lb 8 oz) diced pumpkin or ½ can (28 oz) ready-prepared pumpkin pie filling
- ★ pinch of salt
- ★ 2 large eggs, lightly beaten
- ★ 75 g (2¾ oz) soft light brown sugar
- ★ 4 tbsp golden (light corn) syrup
- ★ 225 ml (8 fl oz) whipping or double (heavy) cream
- ★ 2 tsp ground cinnamon
- ★ 1 tsp ground mixed spice
- ★ ½ tsp ground ginger
- ★ 1 tsp icing (confectioners') sugar

Brandied Egg-Nog

This creamy holiday beverage has Scandinavian and American origins. It is wonderful as a warming evening fireside treat, but is incredibly rich, so should be served in small quantities. It can also be served cold.

1. Pour the milk into a heavy-based saucepan. Add the cinnamon stick and nutmeg. Very slowly bring to the boil.

2. Meanwhile, whisk the eggs and sugar in a bowl until frothy and pale. When the milk is boiling, pour it over the egg mixture, whisking all the time (reserve the cinnamon stick in the pan).

3. Pour the mixture back into the pan and cook over a low heat, stirring all the time until it thickens a little. Do not overheat the mixture or it will curdle. Remove the cinnamon stick.

4. Divide the brandy between warmed heatproof glasses or mugs. Ladle the egg-nog mixture over, then stir before sprinkling the tops with a little cocoa powder or nutmeg. Serve straight away.

SERVES 6

- ★ 900 ml (1¹/₂ pints) whole milk
- ★ 1 cinnamon stick
- ★ ¹/₄ tsp freshly grated nutmeg
- ★ 4 eggs
- ★ 50 g (1³/₄ oz) caster (superfine) sugar
- ★ 150 ml (5 fl oz) brandy
- ★ cocoa powder or extra grated nutmeg, for dusting

Tip

If preferred, dark rum may be used instead of brandy.

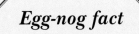

Egg-nog fact

The origin of the word 'egg-nog' is contentious. Some say that the 'nog' comes from 'noggin' – a Middle English term for a small wooden mug used to serve alcohol in taverns – and others say that 'egg-nog' comes from 'egg'n'grog' – grog being the diluted rum that was served on naval vessels.

Mulled Wine

On a cold winter evening, there is nothing more welcoming than a glass of warm spiced wine when guests arrive. The basic mixture can be made several hours in advance and left in a covered pan, ready to warm when needed.

SERVES 8

- ★ 50 g (1³/4 oz) demerara or granulated sugar
- ★ 200 ml (7 fl oz) boiling water
- ★ 2 small oranges, preferably unwaxed
- ★ 8 whole cloves
- ★ 1 stick cinnamon
- ★ 2 bottles medium to full-bodied fruity red wine
- ★ about 75 ml (2¹/2 fl oz) brandy or fruit liqueur, such as Grand Marnier or cherry brandy

1. Put the sugar in a large heavy-based saucepan and pour over the boiling water. Heat gently, stirring until the sugar has dissolved.

2. Rinse the oranges, then press the cloves into one and add it to the pan with the cinnamon and wine.

3. Halve and slice the remaining orange and add to the pan. Warm over a gentle heat until steaming hot (do not boil or the alcohol will evaporate), then turn off the heat and leave until about 15 minutes before you are ready to serve.

4. Add the brandy or fruit liqueur and re-heat until hot. Ladle into heatproof glasses and serve.

VARIATION:
Cranberry and Apple Punch

For a non-alcoholic alternative, use granulated sugar for the syrup. Leave out the clove-studded orange and instead add a 5 cm (2 in) piece of fresh root ginger, peeled and thinly sliced. Substitute 750 ml (1¹/4 pints) each of cranberry juice and clear apple juice for the wine and brandy or liqueur.

Tips

Taste the mulled wine and adjust the flavourings if desired.
You can use up to double the amount of water without spoiling the flavour,
sweeten with a little honey or add flavourings such as sliced fresh ginger, lemon
slices and a bay leaf. Add a dash more brandy or liqueur if liked.

❧

Avoid adding too many orange slices to each glass when serving as it
makes it difficult to drink.

Crafts

Felt Tree Decorations

*The most basic of
embroidery skills are all that's required
to make these three-dimensional felt tree
decorations. Simple shapes are cut, folded, then
blanket stitched together and finished with
a tiny golden bell.*

MATERIALS

For each decoration:

- ★ 30 x 30 cm (12 x 12 in) square of green felt
- ★ 30 x 30 cm (12 x 12 in) square of red felt
- ★ red embroidery silk
- ★ green embroidery silk
- ★ 30 cm (12 in) gold cord
- ★ small gold bell

EQUIPMENT

- ★ tracing paper and pencil
- ★ scissors
- ★ embroidery needle

1. Trace off the ball, bell and star templates given on page 116. Cut out two green and two red larger felt shapes, plus two green and two red small star shapes for the bell decoration and two green and two red large star shapes for the ball decoration.

2. Place the two large green shapes together and stitch together down the centre using red embroidery silk and a small running stitch.

3. Now open up the two layers and press the seam flat using your fingers. Lay a large red shape onto the green felt and pin the edges together. Stitch through the centre using green embroidery silk and a small running stitch, as before.

4. Turn over the piece, then pin and stitch on the remaining large red shape in the same fashion.

5. Apply the four star shapes to the decorations in the same way, placing the red stars on the green shapes, stitching them on with green embroidery silk, and placing the green stars on the red shapes, stitching with red embroidery silk.

6. Using green embroidery silk, blanket stitch neatly around the outside edges of the large shapes.

7. Fold the cord in half and tie the ends in a knot. Stitch the loop to the top of the decoration.

8. Finally, sew on a golden bell to the base.

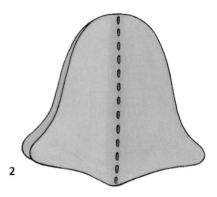

2

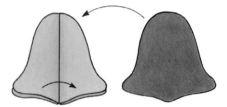

3

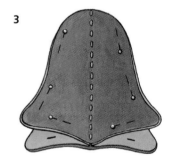

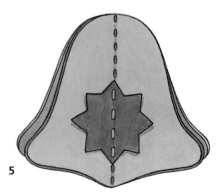

5

Tartan
Padded Shapes

These simple padded shapes are
a very traditional adornment to any Christmas tree.
They can be left plain or embellished with tiny
glass beads along the piped edge and a golden
tinkling bell at the base.

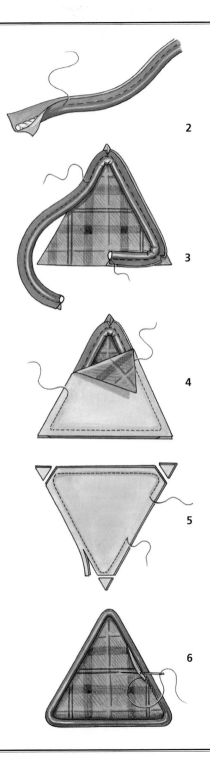

1. Trace off the templates on page 117 for the heart, circle and tree shapes. Cut out two shapes from tartan fabric for each decoration.

2. To make the contrast piping, wrap the red bias binding around the piping cord and tack together.

3. Place the piping onto the right side of one fabric piece, matching the raw edge of the binding with the raw edge of the fabric. Tack close to the piping cord and overlap the ends neatly.

4. Place the other fabric piece on top of the first with right sides facing together. Stitch around the outside taking a 1.5 cm (½ in) seam allowance. If using a sewing machine, you will need to use a piping foot on your machine in order to stitch close to the piping cord. Leave a small gap in the stitching so you can turn the shape through to the right side.

5. Trim the seam allowance down by half, then clip into the curved edges and snip across the points. This reduces the bulk of the seam allowance and ensures a smooth seam when the shapes are turned to the right side.

6. Now turn the shape through to the right side and stuff with toy filling. Slip stitch the gap in the seam.

7. Sew a row of beads along the edge of the piping for added sparkle, then sew a tiny golden bell on the bottom. Fold the gold cord in half, tie the ends in a knot, then stitch the loop to the top of the decoration, ready to hang on a tree.

MATERIALS
For each decoration:

★ 20 x 20 cm (8 x 8 in) square of silk tartan fabric
★ 40 cm (16 cm) red bias binding
★ 40 cm (16 in) piping cord
★ sewing thread
★ about 20 g (¾ oz) toy filling
★ about 50 small glass beads
★ 1 small gold bell
★ 30 cm (12 in) gold cord

EQUIPMENT
★ tracing paper and pencil
★ scissors
★ needle

Angels and Reindeer Decorations

*Add a homespun touch to your
Christmas tree this year with these simple
festive shapes. The pieces of felt are simply glued
together and finished with beads, wire and a
pretty heart-shaped shell buttons.*

MATERIALS

For each angel:

★ 15 x 15 cm (6 x 6 in) square of pink felt

★ 15 x 15 cm (6 x 6 in) square of grey felt

★ 15 x 15 cm (6 x 6 in) square of white felt

★ 15 cm (6 in) gold wire

★ sewing thread

★ fabric adhesive

★ 1 heart-shaped shell button

★ 2 clear seed beads

★ 30 cm (12 in) length of narrow white ribbon

EQUIPMENT

★ tracing paper and pencil

★ scissors

★ needle

★ small pliers (optional)

Angels

1. Trace off the angel templates given on page 118. For each decoration, cut out two main body shapes from the pink felt, two dress shapes from the grey felt and one set of wings from the white felt.

2. Bend the wire into a halo shape, by winding into a circle and twisting the wire ends around each other, folding over at the ends, as in the illustration.

3. Place one of the body shapes on your work surface, then place the halo into position at the top of the head. Hold the wire in place with a few hand stitches.

4. Apply fabric adhesive to the body shapes, then lay the second shape on top of the first, hiding the join of the halo.

5. Glue the two dress pieces into position on the front and back of the angel. Now sew a heart-shaped button to the chest, securing the wings to the back at the same time. Sew on the two clear seed beads on the face to make eyes.

6. Finish the decoration by creating a hanging loop. Fold the length of white ribbon in half, then stitch the ends to the top of angel's head.

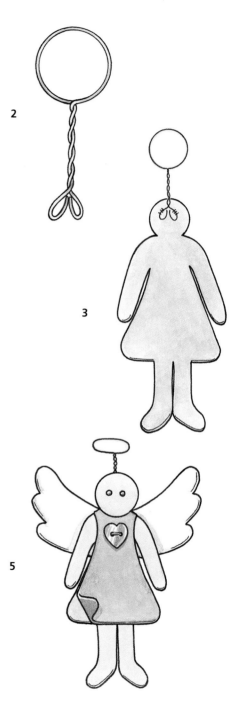

Reindeer

1. Trace off the reindeer templates given on page 118. For each decoration, cut out two body shapes the from brown felt, eight hoof shapes from the dark brown felt and two nose shapes from the red felt.

2. Bend short lengths of wire into a pair of antler shapes, following the illustration. You may wish to use small pliers for the difficult antler shapes.

3. Place one of the body shapes on your work surface, then place the antlers into position at the top of the head. Hold the wire in place with a few hand stitches.

4. Apply fabric adhesive to the body shapes, then lay the second shape on top of the first, hiding the join of the antlers.

5. Sew a heart-shaped button onto one side of the reindeers' body and two black seed beeds on either side of its head to make eyes. Glue on the two red nose shapes and the eight hooves on either side of the reindeer.

6. Fold the gold cord in half, then stitch the ends to the top of the reindeer's back.

MATERIALS

For each reindeer:

★ 20 x 20 cm (8 x 8 in) square of brown felt

★ scrap of dark brown felt

★ scrap of red felt

★ 30 cm (12 in) gold wire

★ fabric adhesive

★ 2 black seed beads

★ 1 heart-shaped shell button

★ 30 cm (12 in) gold cord

EQUIPMENT

★ tracing paper and pencil

★ scissors

★ needle

★ small pliers (optional)

Star Tree Topper

It is traditional to place a star at the top of the Christmas tree. This star design is based on the sawdust-packed fabric pincushions popular in Victorian times. These were made from fabric and decorated with sequins, beads, charms and pretty faux or real jewels and pearls, all held in place with pins. In this modern version, the six-sided star is patched together and embellished with ribbon, sequins and seed beads.

MATERIALS

- ★ 30 x 50 cm (12 x 20 in) piece of heavy iron-on lining
- ★ 50 x 80 cm (20 x 31 in) piece of suitable fabric
- ★ polyester wadding
- ★ 165 cm (65 in) length of 5 cm (2 in) wide gold ribbon
- ★ 20 cm (8 in) length 2 cm ($^3/_4$ in) wide gold lace
- ★ about 300 white seed beads
- ★ 6 gold flower sequins
- ★ 6 gold seed beads
- ★ gold sequins

EQUIPMENT

- ★ scissors
- ★ needle and thread
- ★ fine needle or beading needle

1. Using the diamond templates on page 119, cut 12 small diamonds from the heavy iron-on lining and 12 large diamonds from your chosen fabric.

2. Place the small diamonds of lining centrally on the fabric diamonds and iron into place.

3. Fold the overlap inwards and trim away the excess material at the corners. Iron in place.

4. Use a needle and thread to sew the shapes into place to form two star shapes, each made up of six diamonds, as illustrated.

5. Next sew the two stars together, leaving an opening, then stuff the star firmly with polyester waddingsew up the opening.

6. The star is now ready for decorating. Use neat hemming stitches to sew the ribbon over the join between the two star shapes, sewing the ribbon completely around the front side of the star, then attaching at the back of the star. This will neaten the edge and give your star a clear outline.

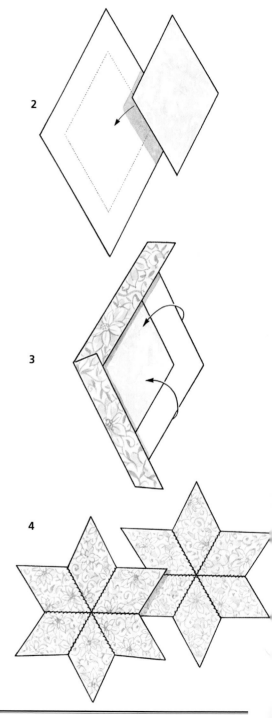

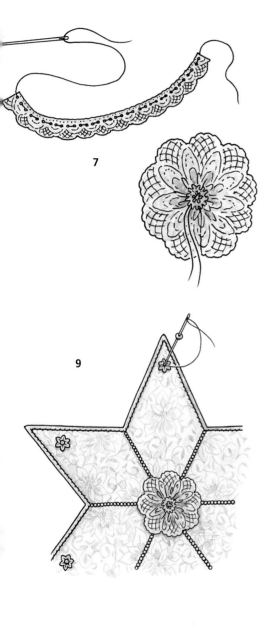

7. Sew a running stitch along the lower edge of the length of gold lace, then pull the thread to gather the lace into a tight circle. Sew in place in the centre of the front of the star.

8. Using a fine or beading needle, sew a line of white seed beads firmly in place along the joins between the diamonds so they are radiating out from the centre of the star.

9. Sew a gold flower sequin in place at the apex of each diamond shape and hold in place with a gold seed bead.

10. Finally cut a small length of ribbon and form a loop. Attach it at the top of the star at the back. Your star is now ready to adorn the Christmas tree.

The Merry Family Gatherings

The merry family gatherings
The old, the very young;
The strangely lovely way they
Harmonize in carols sung.
For Christmas is tradition time
Traditions that recall
The precious memories down the years,
The sameness of them all

- Helen Lowrie Marshall -

Paper Lanterns

*These pretty lanterns look great
lined up in a row to illuminate a mantelpiece
or window sill. They are made using layers of
coloured paper over a glass jar and a candle.
The size of paper needed depends
on the size of your glass container; make sure
you have enough paper to wrap around your glass
with extra room at the top.*

MATERIALS

For each lantern:

★ straight-sided glass jar or tumbler
★ gold, white or printed tissue paper
★ double-sided tape
★ patterned gold or silver wrapping paper
★ thin gold or silver card
★ tea lights or candles

EQUIPMENT

★ scissors
★ metal ruler
★ craft knife

Tip

You can make smaller matching tree decorations, omitting the candle, in order to continue the theme; simply form the lantern in the same way but use a tube of card as the central support.

Never leave a lighted candle unattended.

❧

1. Measure the circumference and height of the glass jar or tumbler. Cut a rectangle of tissue paper that is the same height as the glass and 1 cm ($^1/_4$ in) larger than its circumference. Wrap the tissue paper around your glass and secure the overlap using a strip of double-sided tape.

2. Cut a rectangle of wrapping paper 1 cm ($^1/_4$ in) larger than circumference of the glass and 3–5 cm ($1^1/_4$–2 in) taller that its height. Lay the rectangle face down onto a safe cutting surface.

3. Measure, mark, and score two parallel lines approximately 3 cm ($1^1/_4$ in) from the top and lower edges. Now cut a series of parallel lines approximately 1.5 cm ($^1/_2$ in) apart, running vertically across the rectangle between the two score lines.

4. Apply a strip of double-sided tape across the top and lower edges, then peel off the backing paper.

5. Wrap the wrapping paper around the glass, securing the lower edge first and overlapping the edges at the back.

6. Carefully match the top edge of the rectangle to the rim of the tumbler. Secure the paper to the tumbler, as before.

7. Cut two thin strips of silver or gold card approximately 1 cm ($^1/_4$ in) longer than the circumference of the glass. Wrap these around the top and lower edges of the lantern and secure.

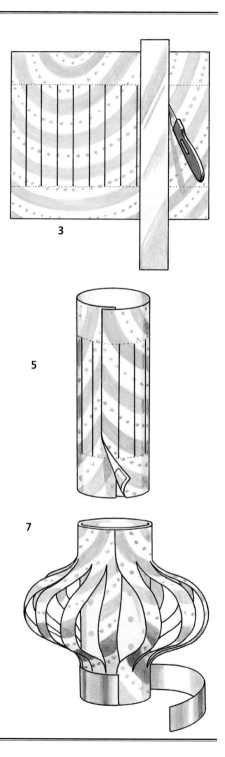

3

5

7

Beaded Glass
Votive Holder

*The gentle glow of candles burning
gives a seasonal feel to a Christmas table.
These simple glass votive holders have been
transformed into something quite magical with
the addition of beads and memory wire,
which keeps its coiled shape.*

1. Measure and cut a 25 cm (9³/₄ in) length of memory wire.

2. Apply a little glue to one end of the memory wire and attach an end bead. This can be a larger or normal-sized bead. Leave to dry until the glue has completely set.

3. Thread the beads onto the wire from the other end, either randomly or in a pattern of your choice until the wire is completely beaded.

4. Apply a little glue to the end and finish off with an end bead. The end beads will hold the beads in place. Leave to set fully.

5. Slip the beaded memory wire onto the glass votive holder and hold in place with a drop of silicone glue.

MATERIALS

For each lantern:

★ at least 1 m (39 in) memory wire

★ strong craft glue suitable for use with wire

★ about 450 mixed beads in red, gold and pearl

★ glass votive holders

★ silicone glue

EQUIPMENT

★ wire cutters

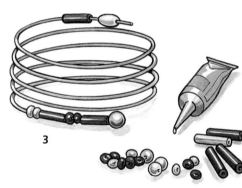

3

5

Tip

Never leave a lighted candle unattended.

~❦~

A Christmas Candle

A Christmas candle is a lovely thing;
It makes no noise at all,
But softly gives itself away;
While quite unselfish, it grows small.

- Eva K. Lounge -

Organza
Gift Pouches

*Anyone would be delighted to
receive a gift contained in one of these
elegant beaded pouches. There are so many
ready-made gift containers available these days,
but a handmade token such as this is a
far more personal gesture.*

MATERIALS

For a bag with round base:

★ 50 x 30 cm (20 x 12 in) piece of green, pink or purple silk organza
★ 50 cm (20 in) piping cord
★ sewing thread
★ 1 m (40 in) length of narrow ribbon
★ about 20 metallic beads

EQUIPMENT

★ tracing paper and pencil
★ scissors
★ needle

Bag with round base

1. Trace off the templates given on pages 120–121, then use to cut out two rectangles and two round bases from the silk organza fabric.

2. Cut a 50 cm (20 in) long and 4 cm (1 1/2 in) wide bias strip from the remaining fabric. Wrap around the piping cord and tack together. Put the two round bases pieces together and tack the piping around the edges, matching the raw edges and neatly overlapping the ends.

3. Place both of the rectangular bag pieces together and stitch down the side seams, taking a 1.5 cm (1/2 in) seam allowance.

4. Fold half of the bag inside out, so the wrong sides are facing together, matching the short raw edges to form a double thickness.

5. Press the fold along the upper edge, then stitch two lines to create a 1.5 cm (1/2 in) wide casing approximately 5 cm (2 in) away from the top fold.

6. Stitch the lower raw edge of the bag to the base. If you are using a sewing machine, you will need to use a piping foot on the machine in order to stitch close to the piping cord. Now turn the bag to the right side.

7. Unpick a few stitches of the side seams between the stitching lines of the casing. Cut the length of ribbon in half and thread both through the casing so that the ends protrude from each side, then trim the ends to neat points. Finally, stitch a small row of beads along seam at the lower edge to complete the bag.

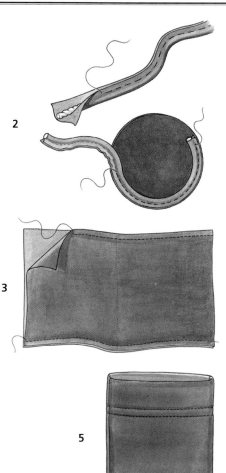

2

3

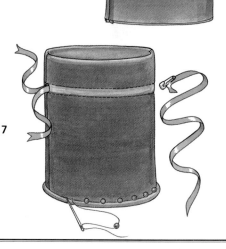

5

7

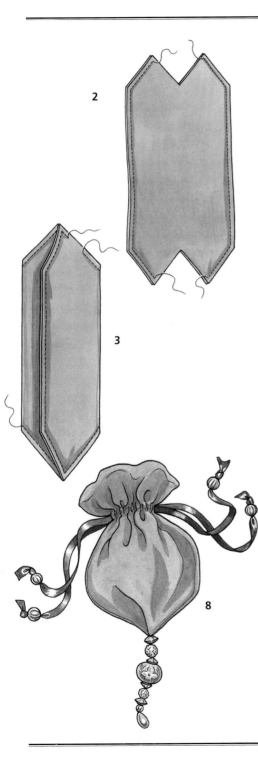

2

3

8

Bag with beaded tassel

1. Trace off the bag template given on page 122, then use to cut out two bag pieces from the silk organza fabric.

2. Place both pieces together, then stitch down both sides to the end points, taking a 1.5 cm ($^1/_2$ in) seam allowance.

3. Join the adjacent short base seams together, leaving a small gap in the stitching so you can turn the bag through to the right side.

4. Turn the bag through to the right side, then slip stitch over the gap in the seam.

5. Push the top half of the bag down inside the lower part to create a double thickness, then press the top fold flat.

6. Stitch 1.5 cm ($^1/_2$ in) wide casing about 5 cm (2 in) away from the fold.

7. Unpick a few stitches of the side seams between the stitching lines of the casing. Cut the length of ribbon in half and thread both pieces through the casing so that the ends protrude from each side. Thread a bead onto the ends of the ribbon, then secure with a small knot. Trim the ends of the ribbon to a neat point or straight edge.

8. To complete the bag, add a few antique gold beads and small glass beads to the pointed base.

MATERIALS
For a bag with beaded tassel:

★ 30 x 30 cm (12 x 12 in) square of green, pink or purple silk organza
★ sewing thread
★ 1 m (40 in) length of narrow ribbon
★ a few antique gold beads
★ a few small glass beads

EQUIPMENT
★ tracing paper and pencil
★ scissors
★ needle

MATERIALS

For a circular bag:

- ★ 40 x 45 cm (16 x 18 in) square of green, pink or purple silk organza
- ★ sewing thread
- ★ 45 cm (18 in) piping cord
- ★ 1 m (40 in) length of narrow ribbon
- ★ small glass beads

EQUIPMENT

- ★ tracing paper and pencil
- ★ scissors
- ★ needle

Circular Bag

1. Trace the template on page 123 for the circular bag, then cut out two bag pieces from the silk organza fabric.

2. Cut a 40 cm (16 in) long and 4 cm (1¹/₂ in) wide bias strip from the remaining fabric, wrap around the piece of piping and tack. Next, tack the piping to the bottom curved edge of one bag piece between the arrows marked on the template, matching the raw edges.

3. Place the second bag piece on top, then stitch the two pieces together around the outside edge, taking a 1.5 cm (¹/₂ in) seam allowance and leaving a small gap in the stitching for turning the bag to the right side.

4. Next, turn the bag to the right side and slip stitch over the gap in the seam.

5. Push the top half of the bag down inside the lower part to form a double thickness, then press the top fold flat.

6. Press the fold along the upper edge, then stitch 1.5 cm (¹/₂ in) wide casing about 5 cm (2 in) away from the fold.

7. Unpick a few stitches of the side seams between the stitching lines of the casing. Cut the length of ribbon in half and thread both through the casing so that the ends protrude from each side. Trim the ends to a neat point.

8. Hand-stitch a row of small glass beads along the piped edge to complete the bag.

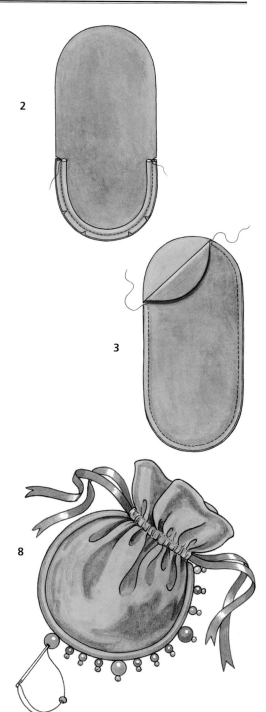

2

3

8

Christmas Past

Each Christmas I remember
The ones of long ago;
I see our mantelpiece adorned
With stockings in a row.

Each Christmas finds me dreaming
Of days that used to be,
When we hid presents here and there,
For all the family.

Each Christmas I remember
The fragrance in the air,
Of roasting turkey and mince pies
And cookies everywhere.

Each Christmas finds me longing
For Christmases now past,
And I am back in childhood
As long as memories last.

- Carice Williams -

Decorated Paper
and Gift Bags

*This richly embossed
homemade gift wrap and gift bag
make an elegant container for any present.
Red paper has been printed with a
repeat stamp design and embellished with gold
embossing powder – a simple technique,
which gives a great result.*

MATERIALS

For a sheet of gift wrap:
★ embossing pad
★ 1 sheet of red paper
★ gold embossing powder
★ sheets of white A4 paper

EQUIPMENT
★ decorative pattern stamp
★ precision heat tool

Gift Wrap

1. Beginning at one corner, apply the embossing pad to the stamp surface, being careful to cover the entire surface of the stamp.

2. Lay the sheet of coloured paper across a clean surface, such as a table top. Press the stamp firmly onto the paper and immediately lift off.

3. Sprinkle gold embossing powder over the stamped area.

4. Shake off any excess embossing powder onto a sheet of white A4 paper. Then pour the excess embossing powder back into the container.

5. Use the precision heat tool to seal the embossing powder, following the manufacturer's instructions.

6. Repeat until you have decorated the whole sheet of paper.

Precision Heat Tool

A heat tool is necessary to fix embossing powder. These tools get extremely hot so do take care. Keep your hands and the paper or card that is being heated a safe distance from the heat source (try holding the paper with tongs). Take care not to singe the paper. Always follow the manufacturer's instructions.

Christmas Cheer

Good husband and huswife, now chiefly be glad,
Things handsome to have, as they ought to be had.
They both do provide, against Christmas do come,
To welcome their neighbours, good cheer to have some.

Good bread and good drink, a good fire in the hall,
Brawn, pudding, and souse, and good mustard withal.
Beef, mutton, and pork, and good pies of the best,
Pig, veal, goose, and capon, and turkey well drest,
Cheese, apples and nuts, and good carols to hear,
As then in the country is counted good cheer.

What cost to good husband, is any of this?
Good household provision only it is:
Of other the like, I do leave out a many,
That costeth the husband never a penny.

- Thomas Tusser -

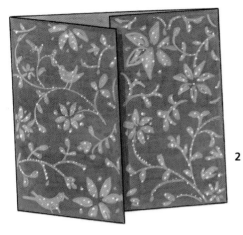

2

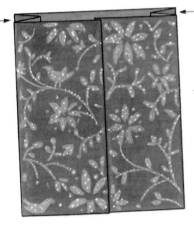

4

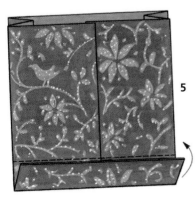

5

Gift Bag

1. Lay a sheet of decorated paper on a clean surface. Use a ruler to measure the length and make a small pencil mark in the centre as a guide.

2. Take one of the short sides and fold it across so it comes about 1 cm ($^1/_2$ in) further than the centre. Then fold over the opposite side so that it overlaps the first side by about 1 cm ($^1/_2$ in). Use glue or double-sided tape to hold in place on the overlap.

3. Fold over approximately 2 cm ($^3/_4$ in) of one of the sides. Press down firmly on the fold. Now fold the opposite side over by 2 cm ($^3/_4$ in) and press down firmly.

4. Open out the folds, then push them inwards, as illustrated.

5. Fold the base of the bag up by 2 cm ($^3/_4$ in) and press firmly along the fold. Make another 2 cm ($^3/_4$ in) fold upwards and stick in place with glue or a strip of double-sided tape.

6. Open up the bag by slipping your hand inside and gently pressing out the corners.

7. Decorate by placing a length of gold ribbon around the bag, just below the top edge. Secure it with glue or double-sided tape, ensuring that the ribbon is pressed down firmly into the folds. Glue a few red sequins around the ribbon.

8. Cut two lengths of gold cord or ribbon for the handles and secure in place on the inside with tape.

MATERIALS

For a gift bag:
- ★ 1 sheet of embossed paper
- ★ glue
- ★ double-sided tape (optional)
- ★ gold ribbon
- ★ a few red sequins
- ★ about 40 cm (16 in) lengths of gold cord or ribbon
- ★ tape

EQUIPMENT
- ★ ruler
- ★ pencil

Stencilled Star
Gift Wrap

*Tissue paper covered with gold stars
lends an air of opulence at this seasonal time.
Children will enjoy lending a hand when it comes
to creating this stunningly simple giftwrap.
Tie gifts with gold ribbon or
yarn and, if inspired, you could stencil little
gift cards to match the wrap.*

MATERIALS

For one sheet of gift wrap:
★ small piece of thin card
★ gold acrylic craft paint
★ scrap paper
★ 2 sheets of dark blue tissue paper

EQUIPMENT
★ pencil
★ craft knife
★ saucer or other shallow container
★ sponge

1. Begin by preparing your stencils. Either draw your own star shapes on card or trace and transfer the star shapes from page 120 onto thin card. Use a craft knife to carefully cut out the stars and cut a 2 cm (³/4 in) border around the stencil.

2. Squeeze a little gold acrylic craft paint into a saucer or other shallow container. Press the sponge into the paint.

3. Practice stencilling with the sponge on some scrap paper to get a feel of how much paint the sponge needs to carry to create the desired effect. Place the template on the paper and sponge the gold paint onto it to create a star. When you are happy with the effect, begin stencilling stars onto one of the sheets of tissue paper. The larger stars look better stencilled quite close together, whereas the small stars can be placed further apart. Take care not to smudge the stars as you stencil across the sheet of tissue paper.

4. Place the sheet in a clean area to dry. This should not take very long, as a minimum of paint is used.

5. Once the paint is dry, the gift wrap is ready to use. Place the remaining sheet of tissue paper underneath the starred sheet for extra thickness, then use for wrapping gifts.

1

3

Once in Royal David's City

Once in royal David's city
Stood a lowly cattle shed,
Where a mother laid her baby,
In a manger for His bed.
Mary was that Mother mild:
Jesus Christ her little Child.

He came down to earth from heaven
Who is God and Lord of all,
And His shelter was a stable,
And His cradle was a stall;
With the poor, and mean and lowly,
Lived on earth our Saviour holy.

And through all His wondrous childhood
He would honour and obey,
Love and watch the lowly Maiden,
In whose gentle arms He lay:
Christian children all must be
Mild, obedient, good as He.

For He is our childhood's pattern,
Day by day, like us, He grew;
He was little, weak and helpless,
Tears and smiles like us He knew;
And He feeleth for our sadness,
And He shareth in our gladness.

And our eyes at last shall see Him,
Through His own redeeming love,
For that Child so dear and gentle
Is our Lord in heaven above;
And he leads His children on
To the place where He is gone.

Not in that poor lowly stable,
With the oxen standing by,
We shall see Him; but in heaven,
Set at God's right hand on high;
When like stars His children crowned
All in white shall wait around.

- Mrs C.F. Alexander -

Holly Napkins

*These table napkins bring a
festive air to the Christmas dinner table.
They are made using decorated
cotton fabric and ribbon, with appliquéd
felt shapes sewn in place in one corner
to make sprigs of holly.*

MATERIALS

For each napkin:

★ four 46 cm (18 in) lengths of 2.5 cm (1 in) wide green ribbon

★ 46 x 46 cm (18 x 18 in) square of patterned fabric

★ sewing thread

★ four 46 cm (18 in) lengths of 1.5 cm (^{1}/$_2$ in) wide white patterned ribbon

★ scrap of green felt

★ scrap of red felt

★ 46 x 46 cm (18 x 18 in) square of plain fabric

EQUIPMENT

★ needle

★ scissors

★ sewing machine

1. Decorate the front of the napkin by pinning the four plain green lengths of ribbon on the patterned fabric square, placing each ribbon 8 cm (3^1/$_4$ in) from the edge of the fabric. Attach the ribbon to the fabric with small neat stitches.

2. Pin the four lengths of patterned ribbon in the centre of the green ribbons. Use small neat stitches to hold the ribbon in place.

3. Using the templates on page 124, cut out three small leaf shapes from the green felt and three large leaf shapes plus three small round berry shapes from the red felt.

4. Pin the green holly leaves on the red leaf backings and into place on one corner of the napkin. Use small neat stitches to hold firmly in place. Sew on the red felt berries.

5. Once the front of the napkin has been decorated, lay it on a clean surface, righ-side up and lay the plain fabric directly on top of the decorated fabric square. Use a sewing machine to sew in place, leaving a 5 cm (2 in) wide gap through which to turn the napkin right side out.

6. Turn right way round and slip stitch over the gap in the seam. Finally, iron the napkin.

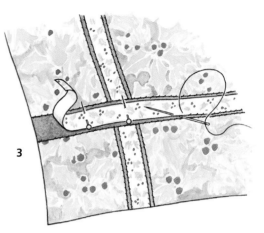

3

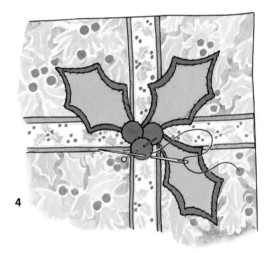

4

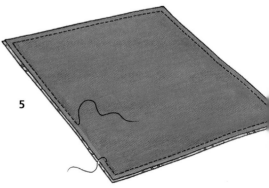

5

Variation: Napkins with Gold Stars

This napkin has been created using fabric paint to paint gold stars onto a white table napkin. Take a white napkin and use the star templates on page 124 to draw stars onto the white serviette using very light pencil. Taking great care, fill in the stars using a paint brush and gold fabric paint. When the pattern is completely painted, set aside to dry. Once it is dry the serviette can be ironed according to the manufacturer's instructions, this will set the dye.

Ribbon
Napkin Rings

Delicately seasonal, these napkin rings
will be a pleasure to sew and will look quite
beautiful on the Christmas table.
They are made from two layers of ribbon and
decorated with cut ribbon, sequins and beads.
If you are unable to obtain the
particular green organza ribbon used you
could use a plain organza ribbon and decorate it
in the same way.

MATERIALS

For each napkin ring:

★ 20 cm (8 in) length of 3.5 cm (1¹/₂ in) wide decorative organza ribbon

★ two 20 cm (8 in) lengths of 4 cm (1¹/₂ in) wide gold ribbon

★ green thread

★ about 10 star sequins

★ about 50 seed beads

★ yellow thread

EQUIPMENT

★ needle

1. Pin the green organza ribbon centrally along one length of gold ribbon. Use small neat stitches to sew in place.

2. Decorate the organza ribbon by sewing on stars and seed beads, as shown in the illustration. Thread each sequin in place, then use a seed bead to hold, sewing the seed bead firmly in place above the sequin. Then sew a row of seed beads above the stars and a row below them.

3. Once the gold ribbon is decorated you can construct the napkin ring. Wind the ribbon round to form a loop. Fold the ends inwards and sew in place.

4. Form a loop with the second length of gold ribbon and place inside the napkin ring to make an inner loop.

5. Sew in place by stitching along the joins using yellow thread. Neaten up any loose edges, sewing the layers of ribbon together.

2

4

Napkin rings fact

Napkin rings were first used in France in around 1800 for identifying family members' napkins in between weekly washes. These useful items soon spread to the rest of the Europe and became decorative to flaunt a family's wealth over the dinner table. Napkin rings were made mostly from silver, but there were also designs in materials such as ivory, wood and porcelain. Since the 1900s, silver napkin rings have become a traditional gift for babies' births, Christenings or Baptisms.

The Holly and the Ivy

The holly and the ivy,
When they are both full grown,
Of all the trees that are
in the wood,
The holly bears the crown:

(Chorus:) O the rising of the sun
And the running of the deer,
The playing of the merry organ,
Sweet singing in the choir.

The holly bears a blossom,
As white as lily flower,
And Mary bore sweet Jesus Christ
To be our sweet Saviour:

(Chorus:)

The holly bears a berry,
As red as any blood,
And Mary bore sweet Jesus Christ
To do poor sinners good:

(Chorus:)

The holly bears a prickle,
As sharp as any thorn,
And Mary bore sweet Jesus Christ
On Christmas Day in the morn:

(Chorus:)

The holly bears a bark,
As bitter as any gall,
And Mary bore sweet Jesus Christ
For to redeem us all:

(Chorus:)

The holly and the ivy,
Now both are full well grown,
Of all the trees that are in the
wood,
The holly bears the crown:

(Chorus:)

Packed Christmas Stocking Card

❦

*Christmas stockings create
a lovely motif and these pretty cards
are created from scraps of fabric,
paper and card. You can pack the stocking
with mini presents, plus a teddy bear charm
and a candy cane, as shown here,
or embellish with your own
unique items.*

MATERIALS

For each card:

★ A5 (5³/₄ x 8¹/₄ in) piece of gold card

★ 8 x 11.5 cm (3¹/₄ x 4¹/₂ in) piece of predominantly green, small-print fabric

★ heavyweight iron-on fabric lining

★ double-sided tape

★ 8.5 x 12 cm (3¹/₂ x 4³/₄ in) piece of red card

★ scrap of red felt

★ scrap of white felt

★ 3D tape

★ scraps of coloured fabric

★ scraps of very narrow coloured ribbons and/or cord

★ craft glue

★ scrap of white card

★ tiny teddy bear button or charm

★ 3 star sequins

★ 4 tiny red jewels

EQUIPMENT

★ scissors

★ red gel pen

1. Score and fold the gold card in half to create the card base.

2. Lay the small-print fabric rectangle on top of the iron-on fabric lining and seal in place with a hot iron according to the manufacturer's instructions. Cut out the fabric rectangle.

3. Use double-sided tape to stick the lining-backed fabric centrally on the red card. Then similarly attach this framed fabric on the front of the gold card.

4. Using the templates on page 124 cut out a Christmas stocking and stocking upper from red and white felt. Iron the red stocking shape onto iron-on fabric lining and cut out.

5. Attach the stocking in a lower central position on the card front using 3D tape.

6. Make little presents by ironing scraps of fabric onto iron-on fabric lining and cutting out two or three small rectangles. Decorate the presents with short strips of ribbon or cord. Either cross the ribbon or cord over the presents and attach on the back with double-sided tape or tie cord around the presents with a bow at the top.

7. Use the candy cane template to cut a candy cane from white thin card and decorate with red gel pen.

8. Use craft glue to hold the gifts in place at the top of the stocking. Glue the tiny teddy bear in place, then stick the candy cane in place using a little 3D tape to create a layered effect.

9. Finally, embellish your card by sticking on sequins and tiny jewels.

3

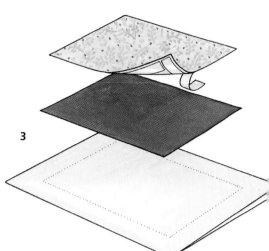

8

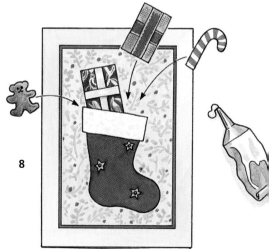

Variation: Stamped Christmas Stockings

These striking cards have been created using a Christmas stocking stamp. Take a
21 x 13.5 cm (8 1/4 x 5 1/2 in) piece of blue card and score and fold in half. Use a black
stamp pad and a Christmas stocking stamp to print a Christmas stocking onto white
card. Sprinkle black embossing powder onto the image immediately after printing.
Shake off any excess powder (taking care to do this over a sheet of paper and returning
any excess powder to the container for future use). Then use a hot air tool to seal the
embossing powder. Repeat with each stocking image, then colour in the stockings using
gel pens. Carefully cut out the stockings and attach in a central position on the front of
the card using 3D tape. Finally, embellish the card with gold star stickers.

Festive Christmas Cards

❦

*Christmas cards first
went on sale in the 19th century but
homemade seasonally illustrated letters
and note cards were being made well
before then. These bright, cheerful cards
can be easily put together with bits
and pieces from both the sewing
box and the craft corner.*

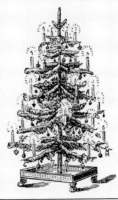

MATERIALS

For each card:

★ A5 (5³/₄ x 8¹/₄ in) piece of red card

★ gold ribbon, at least 15 cm (6 in) in length

★ double-sided tape

★ scrap of white glitter card

★ scrap of red card

★ scrap of dark green card

★ Christmas tree, angel or other seasonal motif

★ A5 (5³/₄ x 8¹/₄ in) sheet white paper

EQUIPMENT

★ scissors

1. Score and fold the red card in half to form the card base.

2. Cut the ribbon to fit the length of the card, then attach centrally down the front of the card using double-sided tape.

3. Cut a 5 x 6 cm (2 x 2¹/₄ in) rectangle of white glitter card, a 5.5 x 6.5 cm (2¹/₄ x 2¹/₂ in) rectangle of red card and a 6.5 x 7.5 cm (2¹/₂ x 3 in) rectangle of dark green card.

4. To create the layered frame, use double-sided tape to stick the three pieces of card one on top of the other. Attach the red card centrally on the green card,

then stick the white glitter card centrally as the top layer.

5. Use double-sided tape to attach the layered frame to the front of the card in a high central position.

6. Stick the motif in the centre of the white glitter card rectangle.

7. Fold the white sheet of A5 paper in half and place it in the centre of the card. Check for size and trim the white paper to fit if necessary. Attach the paper to the inside of the card using double-sided tape.

4

7

O Christmas Tree!

O Christmas Tree! O Christmas Tree!
Thy leaves are so unchanging;
O Christmas Tree! O Christmas Tree!
Thy leaves are so unchanging;
Not only green when summer's here,
But also when 'tis cold and drear.
O Christmas Tree! O Christmas Tree!
Thy leaves are so unchanging!

O Christmas Tree! O Christmas Tree!
Thy candles shine so brightly!
O Christmas Tree! O Christmas Tree!
Thy candles shine so brightly!
From base to summit, gay and bright,
There's only splendour for the sight.
O Christmas Tree! O Christmas Tree!
Thy candles shine so brightly!

O Christmas Tree! O Christmas Tree!
Much pleasure thou can'st give me;
O Christmas Tree! O Christmas Tree!
Much pleasure thou can'st give me;
How often has the Christmas tree
Afforded me the greatest glee!
O Christmas Tree! O Christmas Tree!
Much pleasure thou can'st give me.

O Christmas Tree! O Christmas Tree!
How richly God has decked thee!
O Christmas Tree! O Christmas Tree!
How richly God has decked thee!
Thou bidst us true and faithful be,
And trust in God unchangingly.
O Christmas Tree! O Christmas Tree!
How richly God has decked thee!

Photographed Holly Cards

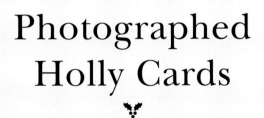

*These stylish cards are made
using photographs of bright holly with
complementary coloured card.
Sprigs of holly have been created
using a holly punch to add extra
decoration and the holly berries
have been embellished with
a little red glitter glue.*

MATERIALS

For a layered card:

★ 27 x 11 cm (10½ x 4¼ in) piece of red card

★ double-sided tape

★ 11 x 9 cm (4¼ x 3½ in) piece of gold card

★ 9.7 x 7.6 cm (3¹³/₁₆ x 3 in) piece of red card

★ 9.4 x 7.3 cm (3¹¹/₁₆ x 2⅞ in) piece of gold card

★ 9 x 7 cm (3⁹/₁₆ x 2¾ in) photograph of holly or other seasonal greenery

★ 3D tape

★ red glitter glue

★ scrap of green card

★ craft glue

★ 12 red stick-on jewels

EQUIPMENT

★ small holly punch

Layered card

1. First score and fold the large piece of red card in half to make the card base.

2. Using double-sided tape, stick the small piece of red card centrally on top of the larger piece of gold card, then stick the smaller piece of gold card in a central position on top of the red layer.

3. Attach the photograph centrally on top of the other layers. The gold and red layers should create a frame around the photograph.

4. Using 3D tape, attach the framed photograph in a central position on the front of the card.

5. Embellish the holly berries in the photograph with red glitter glue.

6. Use a holly punch to press out four holly springs from the scrap of green card. Glue a spring of holly on each corner of the frame.

7. Attach three red stick-on jewels to each sprig of holly as berries.

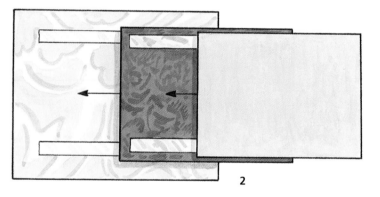

2

4

Window Card

1. Stick the photograph in place behind the window of the card using strips of double-sided tape.

2. Embellish the holly berries in the photograph with red glitter glue.

3. Decorate the card by outlining the oval shape around the photograph with a gold gel pen. You can embellish this further by sticking on a row of red stick-on jewels around the gold oval or by adding a green oval shape next to the gold oval.

4. If you like, you can create holly sprigs by punching out shapes from green card with a holly punch. Stick a sprig in each corner of the card and add three red stick-on jewels to each as holly berries.

MATERIALS
For a window card:
- ★ suitable photograph of holly or other seasonal greenery
- ★ red or green oval window card base
- ★ double-sided tape
- ★ red glitter glue
- ★ red stick-on jewels
- ★ green card (optional)

EQUIPMENT
- ★ gold gel pen
- ★ green gel pen (optional)
- ★ small holly punch (optional)

Away in a Manger

Away in a manger, no crib for a bed
The little Lord Jesus laid down His sweet head.
The stars in the bright sky looked down where He lay,
The little Lord Jesus asleep on the hay.

The cattle are lowing, the Baby awakes,
But little Lord Jesus no crying He makes.
I love Thee, Lord Jesus, look down from the sky,
And stay by my side until morning is nigh.

Be near me, Lord Jesus, I ask Thee to stay
Close by me forever, and love me, I pray.
Bless all the dear children in Thy tender care,
And take us to heaven, to live with Thee there.

Paper Chains

At Christmas time Victorian families
decorated their homes with brightly coloured
paper chains. Bring your own family together
to make these traditional decorations – this is
a perfect project to do with young children.
Here a simple three-colour scheme in gold,
red and green has been used for a
classic seasonal look.

MATERIALS

For one chain, approx 150 cm (60 in) long:

★ 1 A4 (8¼ x 11½ in) sheet of gold coloured paper

★ 1 A4 (8¼ x 11½ in) sheet of green coloured paper

★ 1 A4 (8¼ x 11½ in) sheet of red coloured paper

★ glue (optional)

EQUIPMENT

★ stapler and staples

1. Cut ten strips, 2.5 cm (1 in) wide and 18 cm (7 in) long, from each of the coloured papers.

2. Take one paper strip and form into a loop. Hold the ends in place with a staple or glue.

3. Slip a different coloured strip through this first loop and once again hold the ends in place with a staple or glue.

4. Continue until all of the strips of paper have been used, either linking the different colours in the same sequence or randomly.

2

3

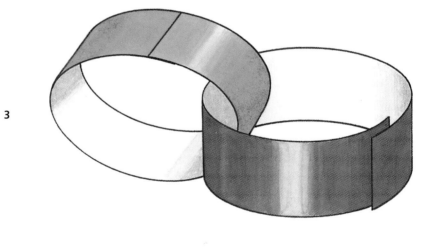

Hanging Garlands

Festoon your home with
vibrant hanging garlands.
Made with long strips
of paper in contrasting colours,
these simple decorations will
brighten up any room.

1. First construct the 'ends' by cutting two 4 cm (1 1/2 in) squares of thin card and two 4.5 cm (2 in) squares of decorative paper. Make a small hole in the centre of each square.

2. Make a loop with one of the lengths of ribbon and push the ends through the hole in one of the thin card squares. Staple in place.

3. Take one of the squares of decorative paper and thread the ribbon loop through the hole in the centre. Pull the paper square down onto the card and hold in place with glue.

4. Repeat steps 2 and 3 with the other square and paper cards and the ribbon.

5. Measure and cut out 4 cm (1 1/2 in) widths of gold and red or green crêpe paper. (The length of these will depend on how much crêpe paper you have.)

6. Lay the green or red crêpe paper strip on your work surface, then lay the gold strip over the green or red one at right angles. Hold in place with four staples, one at each corner.

7. Fold the green strip over the gold strip, then fold the gold strip over the green one. Repeat this sequence until all of the paper is used up.

8. Hold the final fold in place with four staples. Then use glue and staples to stick the 'ends' in place. Gently pull out your completed garland and it should be ready to hang.

MATERIALS

For one garland:

★ A5 piece of thin card
★ A5 sheet of decorative paper
★ glue
★ two 15 cm (6 in) lengths of narrow red ribbon
★ gold crêpe paper
★ red or green crêpe paper

EQUIPMENT

★ scissors
★ stapler and staples
★ ruler

Holly
Christmas Wreath

A holly wreath decorated with ribbon
ornaments and hanging on the front door offers
visitors a jolly Christmas welcome. This
wreath is constructed on a wire and straw base
but, if you prefer, it is possible to use a commercial
wire wreath shape and decorate as you like with
berries, greenery and other embellishments. It is
worth using artificial holly berries in addition to
those on the sprigs since they never seem to be as
many holly berries as one would like. Moss can be
found in garden centres and florists.

MATERIALS

For each wreath:

★ about 4 m (4½ yds) sturdy florists' wire

★ straw

★ moss

★ holly sprigs

★ lengths of florists' wire (optional)

★ artificial holly berries

★ 1 m (3¼ ft) of 3 cm (1¼ in) wide gold ribbon

EQUIPMENT

★ wire cutters

1. Begin by shaping a 35 cm (3¾ in) wide hoop from wire.

2. Take hanks of straw and shape around the wire hoop. Hold in place with wire wound round and round. This will give you a substantial base on which to wire the holly sprigs.

3. Next cover the straw and wire hoop with moss. Once again hold in place with florists' wire.

4. Now, one by one, push the holly sprigs into place, using the wire to hold. You may need to use individual lengths of florists' wire to secure the holly. Continue until the wreath is fully covered.

5. Using artificial holly berries, embellish the holly to your satisfaction.

6. Finally, attach a lovely golden ribbon bow at the bottom, and your wreath is ready to hang up on the front door.

2

4

Wreath facts

*The widespread use of wreaths as a Christmas decoration
dates back to the early 19th Century, when the ancient Germanic tradition
of collecting together evergreen branches during the winter months was
popularised by the Protestant and Catholic churches and rapidly spread across
Northern Europe, Spain and Italy.
For the pre-Christian people this greenery was traditionally
believed to represent a sign of hope through the dark, cold months, and
today the wreath still symbolises the triumph of life and the everlasting light of
Christ during the festive celebrations.*

Variation: Vine and Berry Wreath

If you have access to autumn vine clippings, you can shape them into a wreath, hold in place with florist's wire and decorate with a selection of artificial berries and green ivy fronds along with a big red organza ribbon bow. To make the vine wreath, wind freshly harvested vine trimmings into a circle shape, winding round and round several times to create a sturdy wreath, tucking in any straggling stalks. You may need to hold the wreath in place with florist's wire. Alternatively you can use a commercially produced vine-trimming wreath. To embellish the wreath, push the berry stalks into the wreath and hold in place with florists' wire if necessary. Wind ivy fronds prettily around the wreath and attach small bunches of berries towards the bottom of the wreath. Finally attach a sumptuous organza bow at the bottom.

Gilded Fruit
Mantelpiece Decoration

*What could be more magical
on a mantelpiece than gilded walnuts and
pomegranates highlighted with thoughtfully
placed candles? Gilding takes a little time but the
result is well worth it. The gold will glimmer in the
candlelight, and this will highlight the natural
colours of the fruit and lush greenery.
When using lit candles, be sure to set them
a safe distance from greenery or other
flammable decorations.*

MATERIALS

★ selection of fruit and nuts
★ size (glue)
★ gold or metal leaf
★ wax or shellac (optional)
★ festive greenery, such as fir
★ tree branches and ivy fronds
★ small red apples
★ candles

EQUIPMENT

★ paintbrushes
★ soft cloth

1. Wipe the fruit and nuts clear of any dust or oily marks. Dry well.

2. Use a paintbrush to cover the fruit and nuts with a layer of size. When applying the size be sure to leave patches of fruit uncovered to allow the natural colour of the nuts or fruit to show once the gold leaf has been applied. Set aside for about 15 minutes or until the size is sticky to the touch.

3. Using clean, dry fingertips or some tweezers, lift a sheet of gold or metal leaf and lay gently over the sticky size. Take a clean paintbrush and gently brush the leaf into place. It should stick well.

4. Holding the embellished fruit and nuts over a sheet of paper, burnish with a soft cloth. Excess leaf will come away. If a permanent result is required you could now wax or shellac the gilded areas, however this is not necessary.

5. Once your fruit and nuts are gilded, arrange the festive greenery along the mantelpiece and then place on groups of gilded fruit and nuts, plus little red apples and candles − move things around until you are satisfied with the result.

2

3

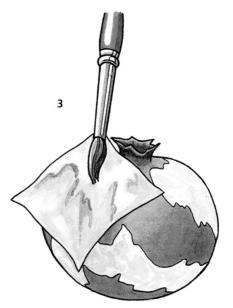

Angelic
Mantelpiece Decoration

*This mantelpiece has been
adorned with art paper in shades of green,
cut in sweeping curves and decorated
with a row of cut-out paper angels and a
strip of gold ribbon.
The angels have been highlighted
with the use of 3D paint, which is easy
to apply and simple to use.*

1. Measure the length of the mantelpiece. Cut a length of the lighter green art paper to fit the mantelpiece, making it 40 cm (16 in) deep. You may need to make a join in the paper to get a long enough run of paper. Fold the top edge of the banner over by 15 cm (6 in); this will go over the top of the mantelpiece.

2. Using a side plate as a template, mark out the scalloped edging onto the card and cut out carefully.

3. Cut out a length of the darker green paper the same size as the light green paper, but a few centimetres deeper. Lay the light green paper on top of the dark green paper so they meet at the top. Secure at the top with double-sided tape.

4. Using a pencil, mark up scalloped edging on the dark green paper; this should follow the scallops on the light green paper and be about 2 cm (³/₄ in) deeper. Cut away the excess paper. Hold in place at the bottom with double-sided tape.

5. Using the template on page 124 and the white card, cut out an angel to go in each scallop.

6. Use the 3D paint to paint a row of dots, 2 cm (³/₄ in) from the edge, along the bottom of the light green scalloped edging. It is a good idea to practise using the 3D paint first on some scrap paper, testing out how quickly and smoothly the paint comes through the nozzle. Use it as if decorating a cake with an icing nozzle. Alternatively squeeze some 3D paint into a small dish and use a paintbrush.

7. Use 3D paint to embellish the angels, following the markings on the template. Set aside to dry; this may take 4 to 6 hours.

8. Once the paint has completely dried, use 3D tape to stick the angels in place.

9. Cut another strip of dark green paper so it is the length of the mantelpiece and 18 cm (7 in) deep. Score and fold to allow a 3 cm (in) overhang. Use double-sided tape to attach it to the upper edge of the light green prepared art paper.

10. Using double-sided tape, attach the ribbon horizontally across the centre of the top dark green strip.

11. Place along the mantelpiece, holding in place with strips of double-sided tape or strategically placed ornaments.

MATERIALS
- ★ A3 (11¹/₂ x 17 in) sheets of art paper in two shades of green
- ★ double-sided tape
- ★ A3 (11¹/₂ x 17 in) sheet of thin white card
- ★ white 3D paint
- ★ scrap paper
- ★ 3D tape
- ★ gold ribbon the length of the mantelpiece

EQUIPMENT
- ★ scissors
- ★ side plate
- ★ pencil
- ★ paintbrush (optional)

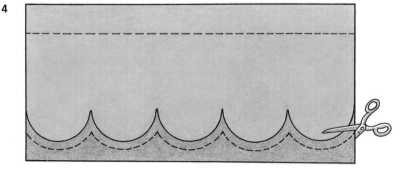

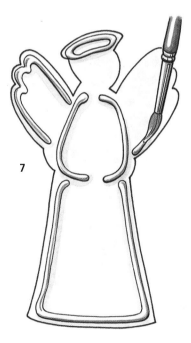

Christmas Stocking

*The custom of hanging
a stocking on the mantelpiece or at the
end of a bed on Christmas Eve is
followed in many homes.
This felt Christmas stocking is
decorated with little felt Christmas trees
and sequins to add a touch of extra
Christmas sparkle.*

MATERIALS

- ★ 30 x 40 cm (12 x 16 in) piece of red felt
- ★ 10 x 15 cm (4 x 6 in) piece of white felt
- ★ 10 x 10 cm (4 x 4 in) square of green felt
- ★ 12 assorted colour sequins
- ★ 5 large gold star sequins
- ★ 23 gold seed beads
- ★ 6 small gold star sequins
- ★ 20 cm (8 in) length of narrow gold ribbon

EQUIPMENT

- ★ needle and thread
- ★ fine needle or beading needle

1. Using the templates on page 125, cut two stocking shapes from red felt, two borders from white felt and four tree shapes from green felt.

2. Pin the four tree shapes to one of the red felt stocking shapes, spacing them out evenly. Using small neat hemming stitches, sew the Christmas tree shapes in position.

3. Decorate each tree shape with three assorted colour sequins and a large gold sequin star at the top. Hold the sequins in place by sewing on a single gold seed bead using a fine or beading needle.

4. Embellish the stocking with further small gold star sequins sewn in place using seed beads.

5. Once the front stocking shape has been decorated you can construct the stocking. Sew a white felt stocking top to each red stocking shape.

6. Lay the stocking shapes together, with the decorated sides facing outwards, and machine stitch around the stocking, remembering to leave the top edge unsewn so that presents can be inserted.

7. Loop the ribbon in half and attach to the top outer edge of the stocking with a few neat stitches. Cover the join by attaching a large gold star sequin and a single gold seed beed.

3

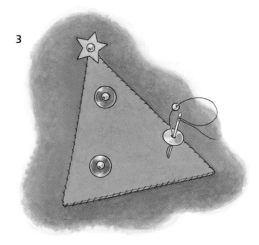

5

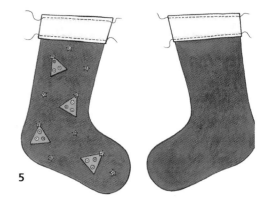

6

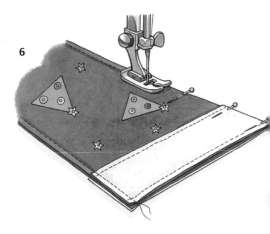

Variation:
Organza and Ribbon Stocking

This stocking is made using the same pattern, but using a decorative organza fabric instead of the red felt and a wide gold ribbon instead of the white border. Sew the two delicate stocking pieces together using ribbon or bias binding.

Stocking fact

There are many legends about how stockings came to be hung at Christmas time. One of the most popular is that a poor nobleman with three young daughters despaired because he had no money to provide dowries for his daughters to get married.
On Christmas Eve the girls hung their stockings over the fireplace to dry and Saint Nicholas, who had heard about their predicament, crept in and put a bag of gold into each stocking. The daughters were overjoyed to find the gold in the morning and were able to get married and live a happy life.

A Visit from Saint Nicholas

'Twas the night before Christmas, when all through the house
Not a creature was stirring, not even a mouse;
The stockings were hung by the chimney with care,
In hopes that St. Nicholas soon would be there...'

- Clement Clark Moore -

Templates

Gingerbread House (pages 22-24)

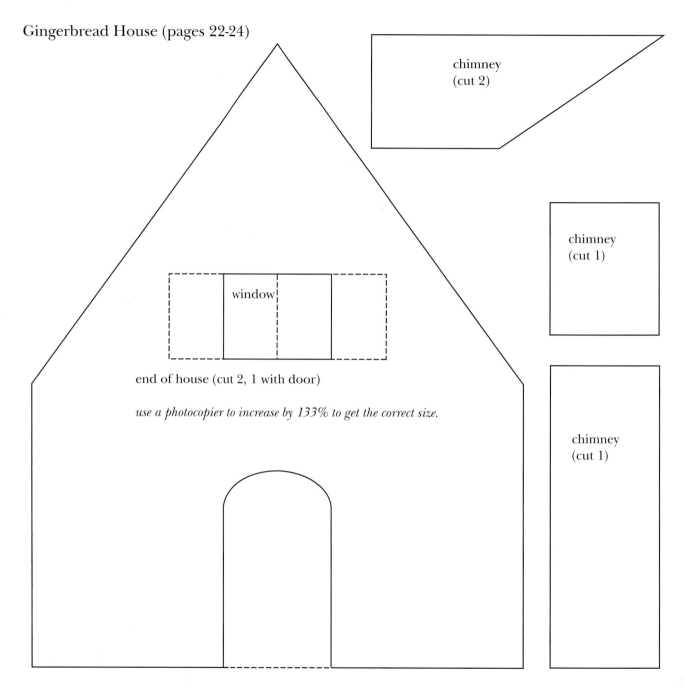

chimney
(cut 2)

chimney
(cut 1)

chimney
(cut 1)

window

end of house (cut 2, 1 with door)

use a photocopier to increase by 133% to get the correct size.

roof (cut 2)

*use a photocopier to increase by
200% to get the correct size.*

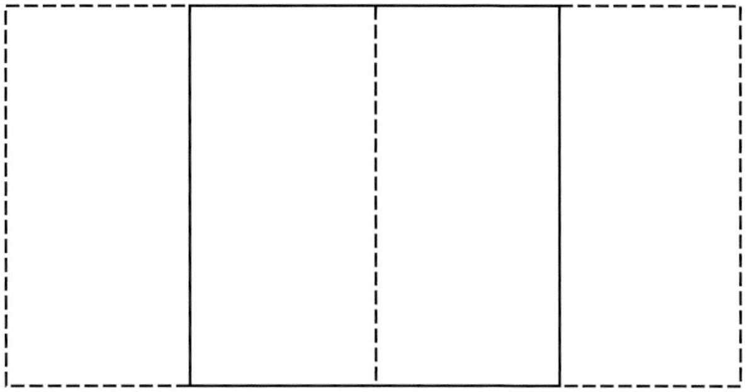

side of house (cut 2)

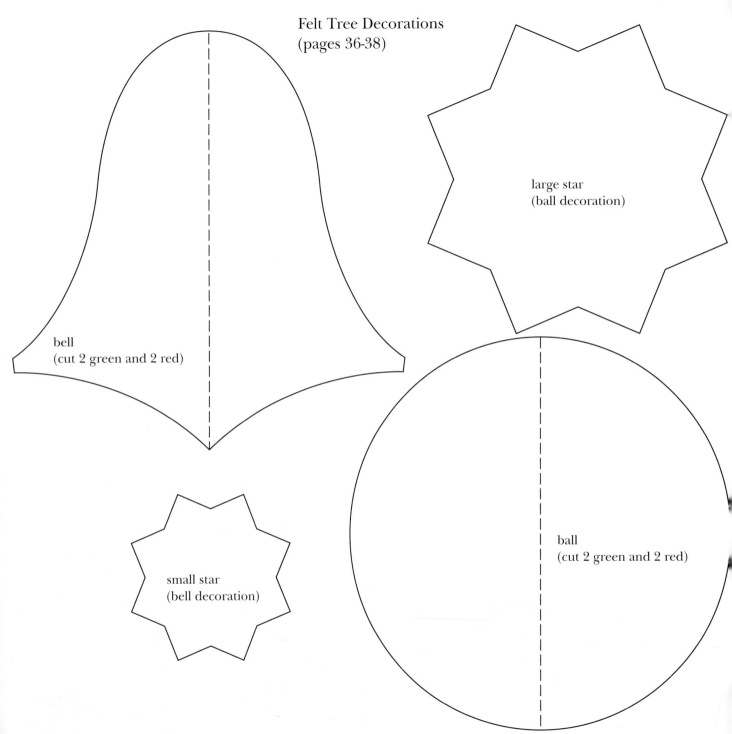

Felt Tree Decorations
(pages 36-38)

bell
(cut 2 green and 2 red)

large star
(ball decoration)

small star
(bell decoration)

ball
(cut 2 green and 2 red)

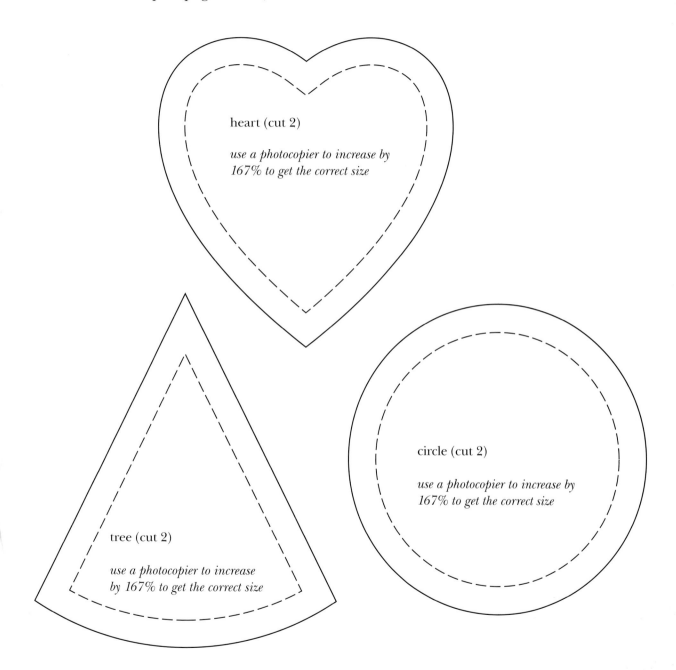

heart (cut 2)

use a photocopier to increase by 167% to get the correct size

tree (cut 2)

use a photocopier to increase by 167% to get the correct size

circle (cut 2)

use a photocopier to increase by 167% to get the correct size

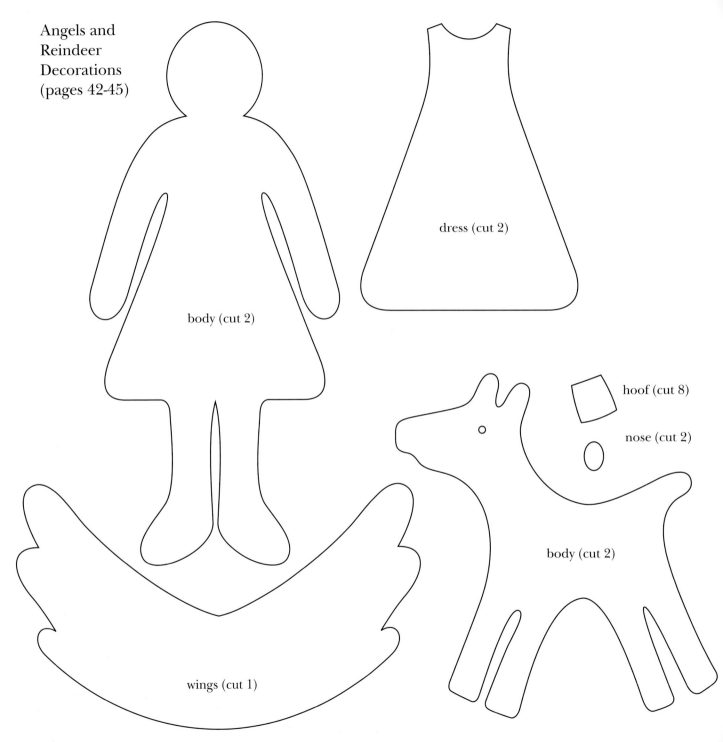

Angels and
Reindeer
Decorations
(pages 42-45)

body (cut 2)

dress (cut 2)

hoof (cut 8)

nose (cut 2)

body (cut 2)

wings (cut 1)

Star Tree Topper (pages 46-49)

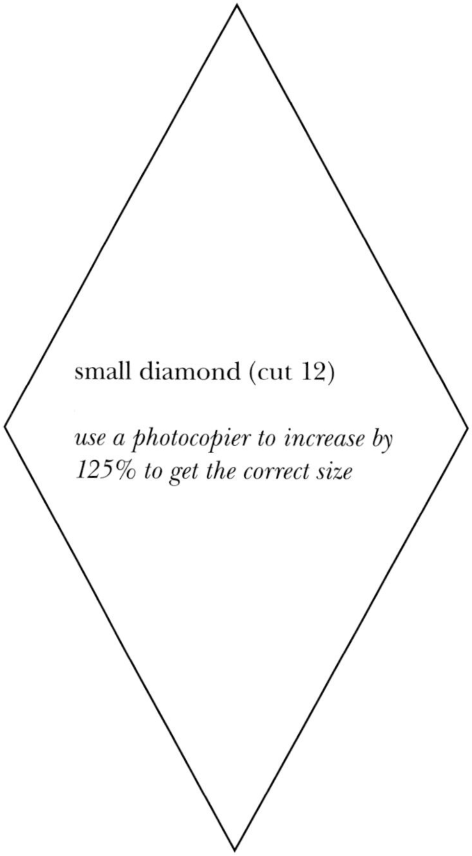

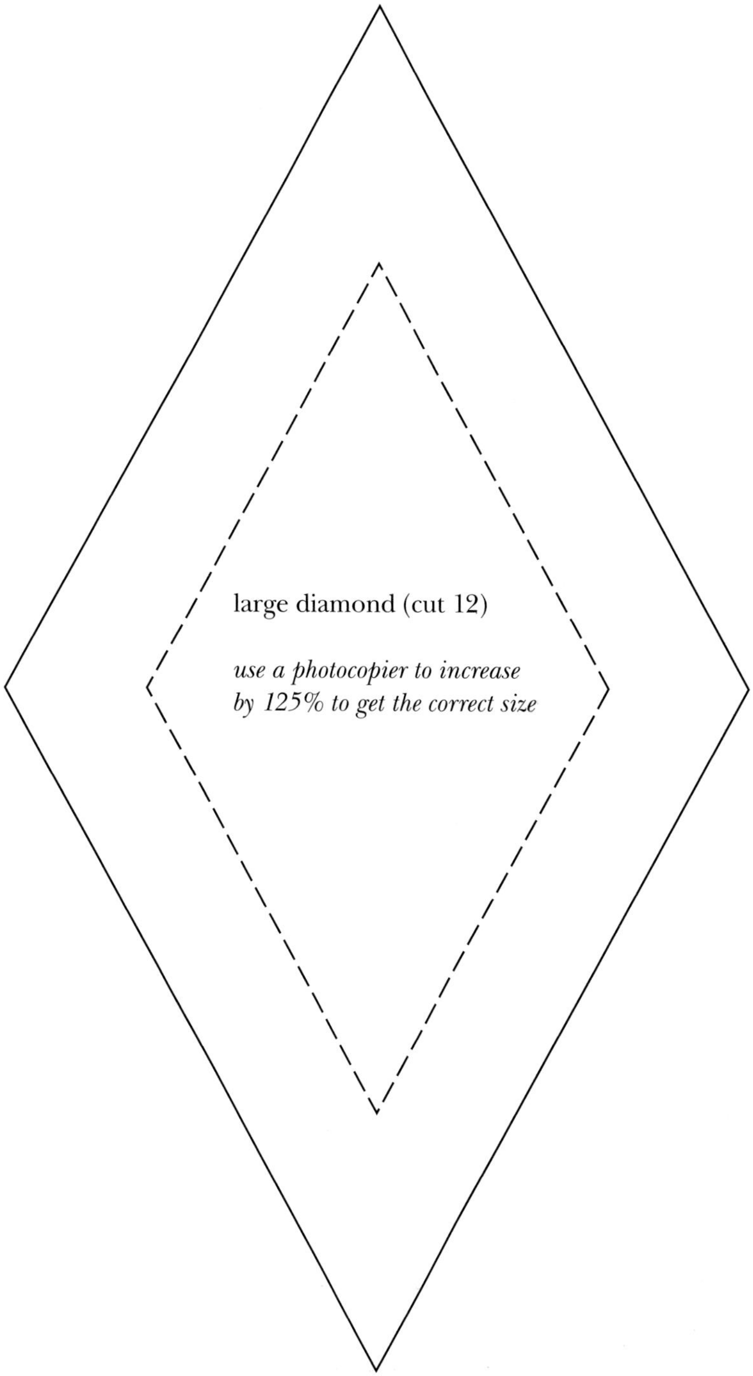

small diamond (cut 12)

use a photocopier to increase by 125% to get the correct size

large diamond (cut 12)

use a photocopier to increase by 125% to get the correct size

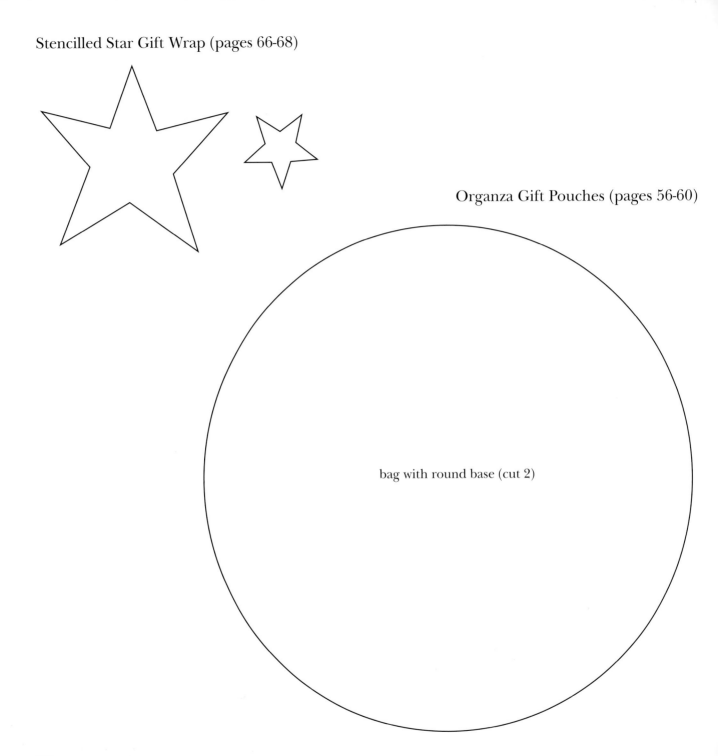

Stencilled Star Gift Wrap (pages 66-68)

Organza Gift Pouches (pages 56-60)

bag with round base (cut 2)

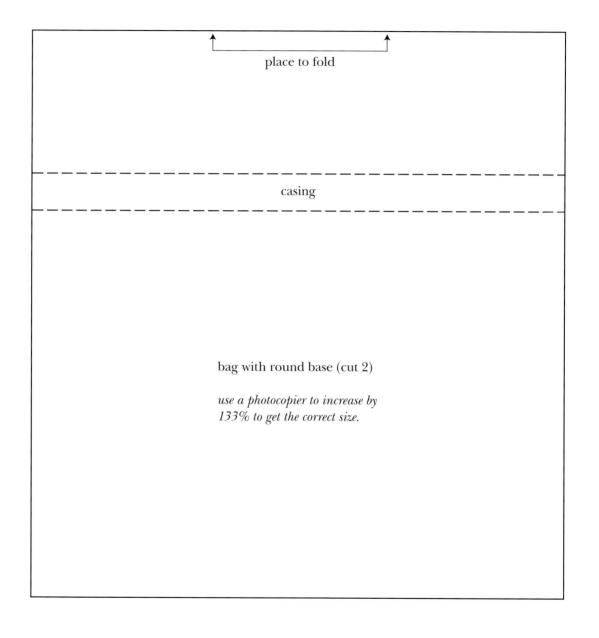

place to fold

casing

bag with round base (cut 2)

use a photocopier to increase by 133% to get the correct size.

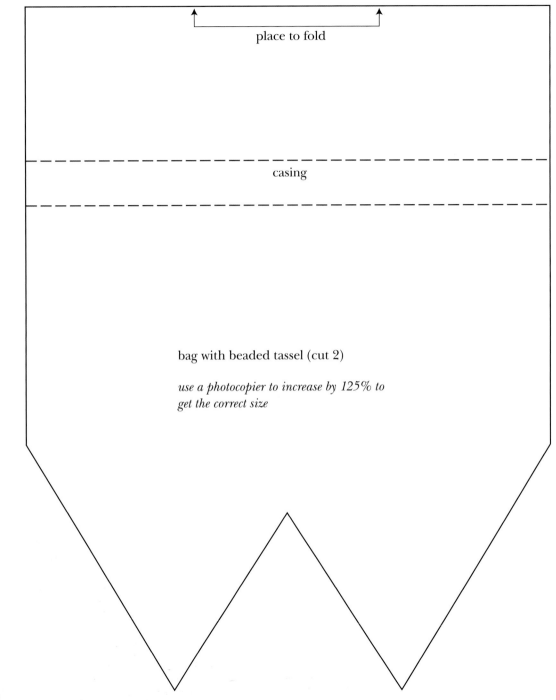

place to fold

casing

bag with beaded tassel (cut 2)

*use a photocopier to increase by 125% to
get the correct size*

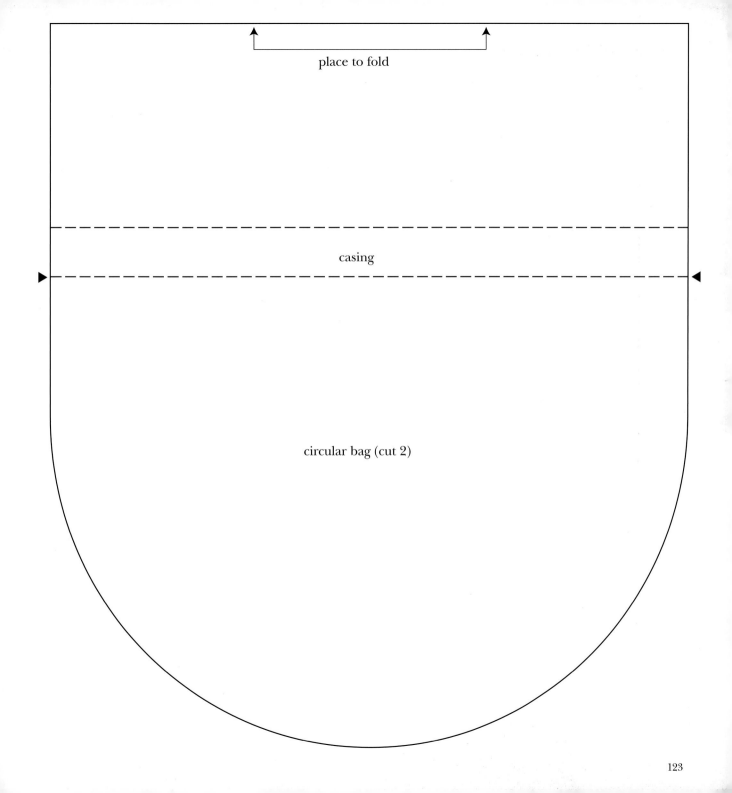

place to fold

casing

circular bag (cut 2)

Holly Napkins (pages 70-73)

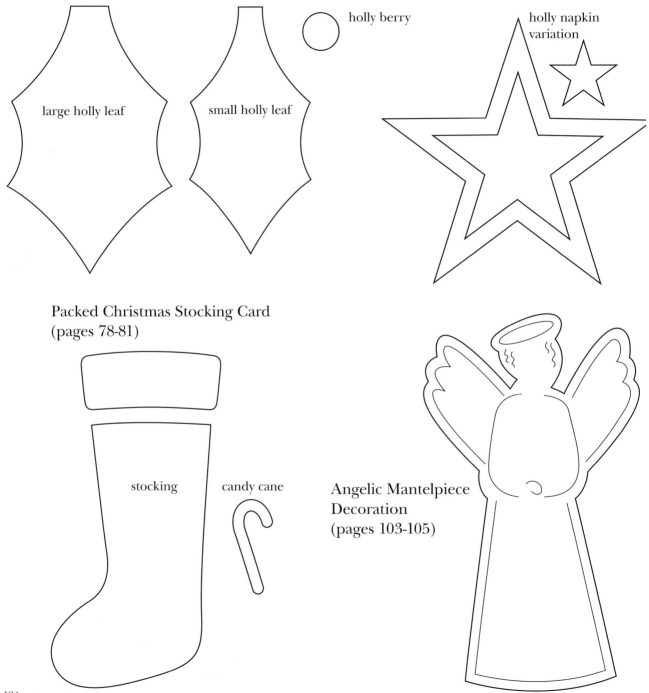

holly berry

holly napkin variation

large holly leaf

small holly leaf

Packed Christmas Stocking Card
(pages 78-81)

stocking

candy cane

Angelic Mantelpiece Decoration
(pages 103-105)

Christmas Stocking (pages 110-113)

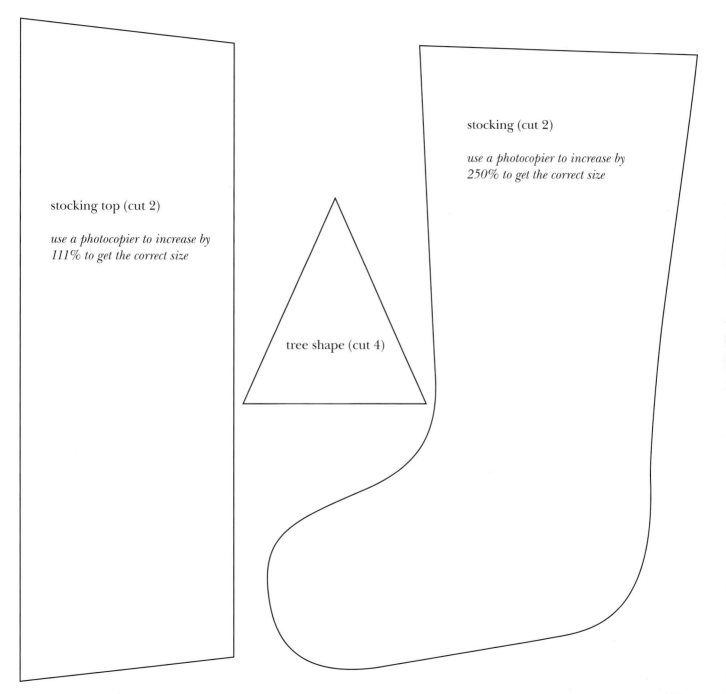

stocking top (cut 2)

use a photocopier to increase by 111% to get the correct size

tree shape (cut 4)

stocking (cut 2)

use a photocopier to increase by 250% to get the correct size

Suppliers

Food, drink and cake decorating supplies

Fornum & Mason
Tel: 020 7734 8040
www.fortnumandmason.com

Lakeland Limited
Tel: 01539 488 100
www.lakelandlimited.co.uk

Majestic Wine
Tel: 01923 298 226
www.majestic.co.uk

Marks & Spencer
Tel: 0845 302 1234
www.marksandspencer.com

Squires Kitchen
Tel: 0845 225 5671
www.squires-shop.com

Waitrose
Tel: 0800 188 884
www.waitrose.co.uk

Decorations, craft and haberdashery supplies

John Lewis
Tel: 0845 604 9049
www.johnlewis.com

Hobby Craft
Tel: 0800 027 2387
www.hobbycraft.co.uk

Sew Simple
Tel: 01603 262870
www.sewsimpleonline.co.uk

Paperchase
Tel: 0207 7467 6200
www.paperchase.co.uk

W.H. Smith
Tel: 0870 444 6444
www.whsmith.co.uk

The Party Store
Tel: 01992 289001
www.partystore.co.uk

Cranberry Card Company
www.cranberrycards.co.uk
Tel: 01443 449776

The Stamp Hut
Tel: 01284 752522
www.thestamphut.co.uk

Index